MOMENTS OF INSIGHT

*the text of this book is printed
on 100% recycled paper*

MOMENTS
OF INSIGHT

The Emergence of Great Ideas
in the Lives of Creative Men

Maria Shrady

HARPER COLOPHON BOOKS
Harper & Row, Publishers
New York · Evanston · San Francisco · London

MOMENTS OF INSIGHT. Copyright © 1972 by Maria Shrady. All rights re-
served. Printed in the United States of America. No part of this book
may be used or reproduced in any manner without written permission
except in the case of brief quotations embodied in critical articles and re-
views. For information address Harper & Row, Publishers, Inc., 10 East
53rd Street, New York, N.Y. 10022. Published simultaneously in Canada
by Fitzhenry & Whiteside Limited, Toronto.

FIRST EDITION: HARPER COLOPHON BOOKS, 1972

LIBRARY OF CONGRESS CATALOG CARD NUMBER: 72-6532

STANDARD BOOK NUMBER: 06-090273-6

Designed by C. Linda Dingler

CONTENTS

Foreword

Ordinarily insights are a dime a dozen. They may make observation intelligent, speech witty, work efficient. But they also may be mistaken, relevant indeed to things as they are imagined, but irrelevant to things as they are.

Great insights do not differ from ordinary ones in any intrinsic manner. Their greatness is due to the fact that they occur at the culminating point of a long series of commonly unnoticed insights. What slowly, and perhaps secretly, has been going forward suddenly or in a brief and intense period comes fully into view. At times the moments of insight set forth in this book are moments of truth or moments of goodness as well. But perhaps the emphasis lies elsewhere. It is on change, discovery, intelligence. These are prerequisites of truth and goodness without necessarily attaining them.

The author has gone far and wide in her striking selection of creative moments. I liked the easy way in which quotations are introduced and informally annotated and the challenge to one's wits set by the non-chronological order of presentation. Many will find the book fascinating. It is good reading, a broad document on a notable feature of the human mind, a repository of great moments in great lives.

BERNARD LONERGAN

MOMENTS OF INSIGHT

GRAHAM GREENE

(1904–   )

Graham Greene has been called an eschatological writer. Death, judgment, heaven, and hell are themes which impart an irreplaceable quality, a fundamental tone to his work. It was, however, not his acceptance of Catholicism that provided him with this focus—his course, it would seem, was marked out immutably from the beginning. At the age of fourteen, touched off by something he had been reading, the moment of vision occurred: He grasped the reality of certain aspects of the human situation, looked around, and saw that it was so. The themes that broke into his consciousness at that time became

SOURCE: Graham Greene, *The Lost Childhood and Other Essays* (New York: The Viking Press, 1951). Copyright 1951 by Graham Greene Selection below reprinted by permission of the Viking Press, Inc. and Laurence Pollinger Limited, London.

the *basso ostinato* of his future work. "Life," as he said, "took on a new slant in its journey towards death."

But when—perhaps I was fourteen at that time—I took Miss Marjorie Bowen's *The Viper of Milan* from the library shelf, the future for better or worse really struck. From that moment I began to write. All the other possible futures slid away: the potential civil servant, the don, the clerk had to look for other incarnations. Imitation after imitation of Miss Bowen's magnificent novel went into exercise books—stories of sixteenth century Italy or twelfth century England marked with enormous brutality and a despairing romanticism. It was as if I had been supplied once and for all with a subject.

Why? On the surface *The Viper of Milan* is only the story of a war between Gian Galeazzo Visconti, Duke of Milan, and Mastino della Scala, Duke of Verona, told with zest and cunning, and an amazing pictorial sense. Why did it creep in and colour and explain the terrible living world of stone stairs and the never quiet dormitory? It was no good in that real world to dream that one would ever be a Sir Henry Curtis, but della Scala who at last turned from an honesty that never paid and betrayed his friends and died dishonoured and as a failure even at treachery—it was easier for a child to escape behind his mask. As for Visconti, with his beauty, his patience and his genius for evil, I had watched him pass by many a time in his black Sunday suit smelling of mothballs. His name was Carter. He exercised terror from a distance like a snowcloud over the young fields. Goodness has only once found a perfect incarnation in a human body and never will again, but evil can always find a home there. Human nature is not black and white but black and grey. I read all this in *The Viper of Milan* and I looked round and I saw that it was so.

There was another theme I found there. At the end of *The Viper of Milan*—you will remember if you once read it—comes the great scene of complete success—della Scala is dead, Ferrara, Verona, Novara, Mantua have all fallen, the messengers pour in with news of fresh victories, the whole world outside is cracking up, and Visconti sits and jokes in the wine lights. I was not on the classical side or I would have discovered, I suppose, in Greek literature instead of in Miss Bowen's novel the sense of doom that lies over success—the feeling that the pendulum is about to swing. That too made sense; one looked around and saw the doomed everywhere—the champion runner who one day would sag over the tape; the head of the school who would atone, poor devil, during forty dreary undistinguished years; the scholar . . . and when success began to touch oneself too, however mildly, one could only pray that failure would not be held off for too long.

One had lived for fourteen years in a wild jungle country without a map, but now the paths had been traced and naturally one had to follow them. But I think it was Miss Bowen's apparent zest that made me want to write. One could not read her without believing that to write was to live and to enjoy, and before one had discovered one's mistake it was too late—the first book one does enjoy. Anyway she had given me my pattern—religion might later explain it to me in other terms, but the pattern was already there—perfect evil walking the world where perfect good can never walk again, and only the pendulum ensures that after all in the end justice is done. Man is never satisfied, and often I have wished that my hand had not moved further than *King Solomon's Mines*, and that the future I had taken down from the nursery shelf had been a district office in Sierra Leone and twelve tours of malarial duty and a finishing dose of blackwater fever when the danger of retirement approached. What is the good of wishing? The books are always there, the moment of crisis waits, and now our children in their turn are taking down the future and opening the pages. In his poem "Germinal" A.E. wrote:

> In ancient shadows and twilights
> Where childhood had strayed,
> The world's great sorrows were born
> And its heroes were made.
> In the lost boyhood of Judas
> Christ was betrayed.

BUDDHA

(c. 560–480 B.C.)

Gautama the Buddha grew up in a world drenched in beauty.
From his father's house, the Himalayas could be seen glistening
in the distance throughout the year, and he enjoyed in every
way the pleasure of his aristocratic milieu. Buddha's father,
wanting to hide the woes of the world from his beloved son,
tried to shelter him from all sorrow but in vain; the thought
of human misery moved his son to grasp the reality of existence
by an insight which, in the normal state of consciousness, transformed his whole view of the world and the self.

Many of the tales of Buddha's eighty years on earth are a
blend of history and myth. The scholars try to arrive at the

SOURCE: *Anguttara-Nikaya* I, 145 *The Maha-Vagga of the Vinaya Texts*
(New York: Time, Inc., 1957).

reality of Buddha by a critical excision of obviously legendary material but there is no conclusive evidence how far the excisions should go. The following selection, however, has the ring of personal experience:

> I was tenderly cared for, brethren . . . At my father's home lotus pools were made for me—in one place for the blue lotus flowers, in one place for white lotus flowers, and in one place for red lotus flowers—blossoming for my sake . . . Day and night a white umbrella was held over me, so that I might not be troubled by cold, heat, dust, chaff or dew . . .

> Endowed, brethren, with such wealth, being nurtured with such delicacy, there came this thought: Verily the unenlightened worldling subject to old age, without escape from old age, when he sees another grown old, is oppressed, beset and sickened. I too am subject to old age and cannot escape it . . .

> While I thought thus, brethren, all pride of youth left me.

> Verily the enlightened worldling subject to sickness, without escape from sickness, when he sees another sick is oppressed, beset and sickened. I too am subject to sickness and cannot escape it . . .

> While I thought thus, brethren, all pride in health left me.

> Verily the unenlightened worldling subject to death, without escape from it, when he sees another dead, is oppressed, beset and sickened. I too am subject to death and cannot escape it . . .

> While I thought thus, brethren, all pride in life left me.

At a stroke, his happiness was shattered and as a result he left home at the age of twenty-nine to seek salvation in asceticism. He practiced rigid mortification for many years but to no avail; it did not bring him awakening. Gradually realizing that mere constraint accomplished nothing, he gave up the austerities of fasting. This was a shocking thing in the eyes of the Hindu ascetics who were his friends. They forsook him, and Buddha found himself alone, practicing pure meditation. As he meditated beneath a Bodhi tree the great illumination came. All at once he saw what is; why it is; how beings are caught up in blind lust for life; how they undergo cycles of birth and death; the nature of suffering and how one can rise above it. He stayed for seven days at the foot of the fig tree tasting the joys of his enlightenment, the clear-sighted vision attained at the highest state of meditation. This insight he uttered as a doctrine in his first sermon at Benares:

> There are two extremes, brethren, which he who has given up the world should avoid. What are these extremes? A life given to pleasures, devoted to pleasures and lusts— this is degrading, sensual, vulgar, ignoble and profitless. And a life given to mortifications—this is painful, ignoble and profitless. By avoiding these two extremes, brethren, I have gained the knowledge of the Middle Path which leads to insight, which leads to wisdom, which conduces to calm, to knowledge and to Supreme Enlightenment . . . It is the Noble Eightfold Path, namely: right views, right intent, right speech, right conduct, right means of livelihood, right endeavor, right mindfulness, right meditation. . .

> This, brethren, is the Noble Truth of Suffering: birth is suffering; decay is suffering; illness is suffering; death is

suffering; presence of objects we hate is suffering; separation from objects we love is suffering; not to obtain what we desire is suffering. In brief, the five aggregates which spring from grasping are painful.

This, brethren, is the Noble Truth: verily, it originates in that craving which causes the renewal of becomings, is accompanied by sensual delight, and seeks satisfaction now here, now there; that is to say, craving for pleasures, craving for becoming, craving for not becoming.

This, brethren, is the Noble Truth concerning Cessation of Suffering: verily, it is passionlessness, Cessation without remainder of this very craving; the laying aside of, the giving up, the being free from, the harboring no longer of, this craving.

This, brethren, is the Noble Truth concerning the Path which leads to the Cessation of Suffering: verily, it is this Noble Eightfold Path, that is to say, right views, right intent, right speech, right conduct, right means of livelihood, right endeavor, right mindfulness and right meditation. . .

As long, brethren, as I did not possess with perfect purity this true knowledge and insight into these Four Noble Truths . . . I knew that I had not yet obtained the highest absolute Enlightenment . . . in Brahma's world. . . . Then I knew, brethren, that I had obtained the highest, universal Enlightenment in the world of men and gods. . . . And this knowledge and insight arose in my mind: the emancipation of my mind cannot be shaken; this is my last birth; now shall I not be born again.

BERTRAND RUSSELL

(1872–1970)

Bertrand Russell has been sometimes compared to Voltaire, and there are indeed numerous parallels that spring to one's mind: The splendidly intelligent head with its witty, mocking lips, the vast bulk and even vaster range of the published work, the voluminous correspondence, the belief in justice and toleration, all that recalls the "Sage of Fernay." But Russell had certain qualities that Voltaire lacked, and one of them was a capacity for experiencing intense moments of illumination which he recorded afterwards with admirable clarity. When it came to writing *Our Knowledge of the External World*, which

SOURCES: Bertrand Russell, *Portraits from Memory* (New York: Simon and Schuster, 1956) and *Autobiography* (*1872–1914*) (Boston: Atlantic Monthly Press, 1967).

remains perhaps the best introduction to his philosophical style and sinuous empiricism, Russell faced great difficulties which he finally resolved by allowing a period of incubation between the first appearance of the idea and its execution. This is far from being an isolated case—it is a process shared by other creative geniuses. Johannes Brahms, describing his method of composing, wrote:

When I have found the first phrase of a song, I might shut the book there and then, go for a walk, do some other work and perhaps not think of it again for months. Nothing, however, is lost. If I afterwards approach the subject again, it is sure to have taken shape. I can now really begin to work at it.*

Ludwig von Beethoven has this to say on the gestatory period:

I carry my thoughts around with me for a long, often an exceedingly long time, until I actually write them down. In this my memory never fails me, so that I can be sure not to forget a theme for several years. I modify, reject, make fresh attempts, until I am finally satisfied. Only then do I begin execution in breadth, height, and depth and since I now know what I want, the fundamental idea never leaves me; it grows, I see and hear it in its entirety and what remains to be done is merely the notation which falls into shape very quickly.

The whole process is summed up most succinctly by Russell in *Portraits from Memory* where he describes how

having by a time of very intense concentration, planted the problem in my subconsciousness it would germinate

* The quotations of Brahms and Beethoven are from Walter Kuhn and Hans Lebede, *Von Musikern und Musik* (Berlin and Leipzig: Verlag G. Freytag, 1938). Translated by the author.

underground, until, suddenly the solution emerged with blinding clarity, so that it only remained to write down what had appeared as if in a revelation. . . .

The most curious example of this process, and the one which led me subsequently to rely upon it, occurred at the beginning of 1914. I had undertaken to give the Lowell Lectures at Boston, and had chosen as my subject "Our Knowledge of the External World." Throughout 1913 I thought about this topic. In term time in my rooms at Cambridge, in vacations in a quiet inn on the upper reaches of the Thames, I concentrated with such intensity that I sometimes forgot to breathe and emerged panting as from a trance. But all to no avail. To every theory that I could think of I could perceive fatal objections. At last, in despair, I went off to Rome for Christmas, hoping that a holiday would revive my flagging energy. I got back to Cambridge on the last day of 1913, and although my difficulties were still completely unresolved I arranged, because the remaining time was short, to dictate as best as I could to a stenographer. Next morning, as she came in at the door, I suddenly saw exactly what I had to say, and proceeded to dictate the whole book without a moment's hesitation.

A formidable moment of illumination, of clear trance, came to Russell in 1901. In his *Autobiography* he tells how several months before this event he experienced a time of intellectual intoxication: "My sensations resembled those one has after climbing a mountain in mist, when, on reaching the summit, the mist suddenly clears, and the country becomes visible for forty miles in every direction." For years he had been endeavoring to analyze the fundamental notions of mathematics.

Suddenly he discovered what appeared to be the definite answer. This intellectually exhilarating period was followed by a shattering experience, which, within a few hours, changed his views on war, education, and the unendurability of human loneliness.*

During the Lent Term of 1901, we joined with the Whiteheads in taking Professor Maitland's house in Downing College. Professor Maitland had had to go to Madeira for his health. His housekeeper informed us that he had "dried hisself up eating dry toast," but I imagine this was not the medical diagnosis. Mrs. Whitehead was at this time becoming more and more of an invalid, and used to have intense pain owing to heart trouble. Whitehead and Alys and I were all filled with anxiety about her. He was not only deeply devoted to her but also very dependent upon her, and it seemed doubtful whether he would ever achieve any more good work if she were to die. One day, Gilbert Murray came to Newnham to read part of his translation of *The Hippolytus*, then unpublished. Alys and I went to hear him, and I was profoundly stirred by the beauty of the poetry. When we came home, we found Mrs. Whitehead undergoing an unusually severe bout of pain. She seemed cut off from everyone and everything by walls of agony, and the sense of the solitude of each human soul suddenly overwhelmed me. Ever since my marriage, my emotional life had been calm and superficial. I had forgotten all the deeper issues, and had been content with flippant cleverness. Suddenly the ground seemed to give way beneath me, and I found myself in quite another region. Within five minutes I went through some such re-

* Selection from *Autobiography* reprinted by permission of George Allen & Unwin, Ltd., London and the Atlantic Monthly Press.

flections as the following: The loneliness of the human soul is unendurable; nothing can penetrate it except the highest intensity of the sort of love that religious teachers have preached; whatever does not spring from this motive is harmful, or at best useless; it follows that war is wrong, that a public school education is abominable, that the use of force is to be deprecated, and that in human relations one should penetrate to the core of loneliness in each person and speak to that. The Whitehead's youngest boy, aged three, was in the room. I had previously taken no notice of him, or he of me. He had to be prevented from troubling his mother in the middle of her paroxysms of pain. I took his hand and led him away. He came willingly, and felt at home with me. From that day to his death in the War in 1918, we were close friends.

At the end of those five minutes, I had become a completely different person. For a time, a sort of mystic illumination possessed me. I felt that I knew the inmost thoughts of everybody that I met in the street, and though this was, no doubt, a delusion, I did in actual fact find myself in far closer touch than previously with all my friends, and many of my acquaintances. Having been an Imperialist, I became during those five minutes a pro-Boer and Pacifist. Having for years cared only for exactness and analysis, I found myself filled with semimystical feelings about beauty, with an intense interest in children, and with a desire almost as profound as that of the Buddha to find some philosophy which should make human life endurable. A strange excitement possessed me, containing intense pain but also some element of triumph through the fact that I could dominate pain, and make it, as I thought, a gateway to wisdom. The mystic insight which I then imagined myself to possess has largely faded, and the habit of analysis has reasserted itself. But something of what I thought I saw in that moment has remained always with me, causing my attitude during the first war, my interest in children, my indifference to minor misfortunes, and a certain emotional tone in all my human relations.

LUDWIG WITTGENSTEIN

(1889–1951)

The Austrian philosopher Ludwig Wittgenstein began his
career as a pupil of Bertrand Russell and ended as his supplanter
at both Oxford and Cambridge. Lord Russell recalls how the
young Wittgenstein who had been his pupil for five terms,
came up to him and said: "Will you please tell me whether
I am a complete idiot or not? Because, if I am a complete idiot
I shall become an aeronaut, but if I am not, I shall become a
philosopher." Russell, who wasn't sure whether he was dealing
with a genius or merely with an eccentric, asked him to write
something on a philosophical subject during vacation. After
receiving the paper and reading one sentence he said: "No

SOURCE: Norman Malcolm, *Ludwig Wittgenstein: A Memoir* (New
York and London: Oxford University Press, 1958).

Wittgenstein, you must not become an aeronaut." And he didn't. He became one of the leading philosophers of his century. Yet his work, if not his name, is little known outside of philosophical circles. The reason for this is obvious—his principal contributions, the *Tractatus Logico—Philosophicus* and the *Philosophical Investigations*, are so difficult as to be virtually incomprehensible to the layman. They also represent two distinct philosophies.

Wittgenstein entered philosophy through the gate of mathematics. When he was serving in the Austrian army during the First World War, he became increasingly interested in the question of the nature of the significant proposition. "My whole task," he writes in one of the philosophical notebooks he kept during the war, "consists in explaining the nature of the proposition." What is the nature of language and its relation to the reality which is described in language? Does language mirror the world? This is how the central idea of the *Tractatus* occurred to him:

> It was in the autumn of 1914, on the East front. Wittgenstein was reading in a magazine about a law-suit in Paris concerning an automobile accident. At the trial a miniature model of the accident was presented before the court. The model here served as a proposition; that is, as a description of a possible state of affairs. It had this function owing to a correspondence between the parts of the model (the miniature -houses, -cars, -people) and things (houses, cars, people) in reality. It now occurred to Wittgenstein, that one might reverse the analogy and say that a *proposition* serves as a model or *picture*, by virtue of a similar correspondence between *its* parts and the world. The way in which the parts of the proposition are combined—the *structure* of the proposition—depicts a possible

combination of elements in reality, a possible state of affairs.

At that time his theory that a proposition was a picture of the world, was considered strikingly original and engaging. In another context Carl Jung has pointed out that only a genius or a madman can so disentangle himself from the bonds of reality as to see, for instance, the world as a picture book. He quotes the example of an incurably insane locksmith:

He had never been blessed with intelligence, but he had, among other things, hit upon the magnificent idea that the world was his picture book, the pages of which he could turn at will. The proof was quite simple; he had only to turn round, and there was a new page for him to see. This is Schopenhauer's *World as Will and Idea* in unadorned, primitive concreteness of vision. A shattering idea indeed, born of extreme alienation and seclusion from the world, but so naively and simply expressed that one can only smile at the grotesqueness of it. And yet this primitive way of looking lies at the very heart of Schopenhauer's brilliant vision of the world.*

It was this "primitive way of looking," combined with a penetrating and fiery intelligence, that precipitated the insight which led to the rich complexity of Wittgenstein's *Tractatus*. After its publication in 1921, Wittgenstein withdrew from philosophy, thinking that he had solved its main problems. But eight years later, after having come to regard this decision as somewhat premature, he returned to Cambridge and began the work that was to culminate in the *Philosophical Investigations*. As suddenly as a map of a diagram had inspired the conception of the *Tractatus*, so a flick of a hand brought about its downfall. Professor Norman Malcolm recounts the incident:

* As quoted in an article by Anthony Storr "Genius—What Is It? Who Has It? *Vogue* March 1971.

Wittgenstein and Professor Sraffa, a lecturer in Economics at Cambridge, argued together a great deal over the ideas of the *Tractatus*. One day (they were riding, I think, on a train) when Wittgenstein was insisting that a proposition and that which it describes must have the same "logical form," the same "logical multiplicity," Sraffa made a gesture, familiar to Neopolitans as meaning something like disgust or contempt, of brushing the underneath of his chin with an outward sweep of the fingertips of one hand. And he asked: "What is the logical form of *that?*" Sraffa's example produced in Wittgenstein the feeling that there was an absurdity in the insistence that a proposition and what it describes must have the same "form." This broke the hold on him of the conception that a proposition must literally be a "picture" of the reality it describes.

This did not mean that Wittgenstein completely repudiated his earlier work; he definitely wanted the *Tractatus* published jointly with the *Investigations* which he kept on revising for the rest of his life. "One day," Professor Malcolm records, "when Wittgenstein was passing a field where a football game was in progress, the thought first struck him that in language we play GAMES with WORDS. A central idea of his philosophy, the notion of a 'language game,' apparently had its genesis in this incident." His aim was still to understand the structure and limits of thought and his method was to study the structure and limits of language. But whereas before he had deduced from an abstract theory, he now was analyzing example after example of linguistic usage. By this he hoped to disentangle the confusions which over-simplified theories could generate.

GERARD MANLEY HOPKINS

(*1844–1889*)

There exists a story about a gardener who found Hopkins on his hands and knees examining a dewdrop; when he returned half an hour later, the young poet was still in the same position, enraptured by what he saw. No doubt it was "inscape" he was searching for, the "thisness" that is both the beauty of an object and the law of its being. Hopkins's sensuous response to nature was perhaps keener than that of any other English poet; but he also sought to know its laws and work-

SOURCES: *Gerard Manley Hopkins. A Selection of His Poems and Prose.* Selected with and Introduction and Notes by W. H. Gardner (New York and London: Penguin Books, 1953) and *Gerard Manley Hopkins. Journals and Papers.* Edited by Humphrey House and completed by Graham Storey. (New York and London: Oxford University Press, 1959).

ings. There are wonderfully exact and delicate descriptions of this in his notebooks. Oaks baffle him at first: "The organization of this tree is difficult," he writes on July 11, 1866, "but I shall study them further." A week later he has the answer and it explains for him the whole being of the tree:

> I have found the law of the oak leaves. It is of platter-shaped stars altogether; the leaves lie close like pages, packed, and as if drawn tightly to. But these old packs, which lie at the end of their twigs, throw out now long shoots alternately and slimly leaved, looking like bright keys. All the sprays, but markedly these ones shape out, and, as it were, embrace greater circles, and the dip and toss of these make the wider and less organic articulations of the tree.

From that time onwards, the journal entries show him feeling his way towards a formulation of his favorite idea: His mind was such that he could not rest content until he had found an intellectual formula to define the process. He calls "inscape" the individualizing force in the object, and "instress" its impact on the mind of the perceiver, an illumination by which the inherent order and unity of external forms is realized. As often happens in the case of creative people, in order to become himself he needed another. What he needed most, was someone to give his pursuit religious, and so, for him, poetic sanction. It happened in August 1872. While he was studying medieval philosophy he came upon the writings of the thirteenth-century philosopher Duns Scotus and in his "principle of individuation, "discovered a corroboration of his own private theory. Scotus attached great importance to the concrete thing, the individualizing form which makes "this man this" and not "that." To this difference he gave the name "haecceitas." Whereas Aquinas had held that the individual was really unknowable, only universals being known, Scotus maintained that the mind could arrive at a direct glimpse of that particular "thisness." Furthermore, it is by this knowledge of the singular that we attain knowledge of universals.

It is easy to imagine the joy Hopkins felt when he realized how close these ideas were to his own. The impact was so strong that from it stem at least a dozen of his best poems. In one of them he calls Scotus "of reality the rarest-veinèd unraveller." Here is the journal entry in which he recalls the actual encounter:

> The ovary of the blown foxglove surrounded by the green calyx is perhaps that conventional flower in Pointed and other floriated work which I could not before identify. It might also be St. John's-wort.
>
> Stepped into a barn of ours, a great shadowy barn, where the hay had been stacked on either side, and looking at the great rudely arched timberframes—principals(?) and tie-beams, which make them look like bold big A's with the cross-bar high up—I thought how sadly beauty of inscape was unknown and buried away from simple people and yet how near at hand it was if they had eyes to see it and it could be called out everywhere again . . .
>
> After the examinations we went for our holiday out to Douglas in the Isle of Man August 3. At this time I had first begun to get hold of the copy of Scotus on the Sentences in the Baddely library and was flush with a new stroke of enthusiasm. It may come to nothing or it may be a mercy from God. But just then when I took in any inscape of the sky or sea I thought of Scotus.

MICHELANGELO BUONAROTTI

(1475–1564)

The case of Hopkins is far from being the only instance of a creative person being awakened to his own genius by that of another. Kenneth Clark recounts such an event in the career of Michelangelo:

> It happened on Wednesday, January 4, 1506, in a vineyard near San Pietro in Vincoli; and within a few hours Michelangelo was on the spot. Pliny's description of the Laocoon group had touched the imaginations of Renaissance artists, and even before its excavation, attempts had been made to draw what it could have been like. Michelangelo, and his friend Giuliano da Sangallo, identified the

SOURCE: Kenneth Clark, *The Nude* (New York: Doubleday, 1956).

newly discovered group immediately. He also recognized that this was the sanction of his deepest need. From the centaur relief onward he had wished to make violent muscular movement expressive of something more than a physical struggle. But he had found little authority for this aim in classic art, which was his only criterion where the nude was concerned. And then, from a subterranean chamber, marvellously intact, there appeared the authority he wanted, the statue that Pliny himself described as a "work of art to be preferred above all else in painting and sculpture." Even at this distance of time there is something miraculous about the whole event, because after centuries of excavation the Laocoon remains an exceptional piece of antique sculpture, and one of the few that does anticipate the needs of Michelangelo.

The result, however, was slow in coming. He had planted the idea in his subconsciousness, where it rumbled around, until, four years later, it emerged in two remarkable figures on the ceiling of the Sistine Chapel. Within the Zone of Heaven, the pair of athletes flanking the Creation of Light, reflect the impact of the Laocoon on Michelangelo's style. The blander forms of antiquity—still visible in the preceding pair—are now abandoned for a treatment that, no doubt, had its roots deeply in Michelangelo's temperament. And yet, without the illuminating experience at the sight of the Laocoon he might have lacked the confirmation needed to develop the full power of his imagination. For the twisted and tortured rhythms of these nudes express in a manner unsurpassed what we have come to consider most characteristic of Michelangelo: the predicament of a human body when inhabited by an immortal soul.

CLAUDE MONET

(1840–1926)

It is hard to believe that the discovery of outdoor oil painting should have happened so late in European civilization: up to the middle of the nineteenth century hardly any painter had finished a canvas on the spot. Constable, of course, had painted outdoor sketches earlier, but they were sketches, meant to be finished later on in the studio. It took Louis Eugene Boudin's enraptured delight in nature to insist on spontaneity in its rendering. These were the precepts Boudin imparted to the young Monet:

> The first impression is the right one, be just as stubborn as you can in sticking to it. Whatever is painted directly, on

SOURCE: D. Rouart, *Claude Monet* (Lausanne, 1958).

the spot, always has a vigour, a power, a vivacity of touch that can't be recovered in the studio. Three brush strokes from nature are worth more than two days' work at the easel.

Here, in a few sentences, was the fundamental principle of Impressionism. Although Boudin himself felt that he lacked "verve of execution," and that perfection was forever eluding him, he handed his gospel on to Monet who later describes his youthful initiation as "a bolt from the blue." He recalls how they both set up their easels at Rouelles, near Le Havre. Boudin quickly began to work while Monet, condescendingly at first, and then more attentively, watched. These were the coastal scenes Monet had known intimately since childhood but now, by a sudden flash, they were transformed for him, and he himself was transformed:

Suddenly a veil was torn away. I had understood—I had realized what painting could be. By the single example of this painter devoted to his art with such independence, my destiny as a painter opened out to me.

The revelation proved to be a two-fold one, both of painting and of nature, each in terms of the other. For the validation of the artistic insight in the artistic deed, and with the exception of a few departures into other fields, Monet's entire body of work was oriented towards nature. He communicated the very pulse-beat of sun-ripe fields and trees and rippled water and enabled us to share, by a certain reenactment, his own original vision.

RICHARD WAGNER

(1813–1883)

Whatever his defects as a human being—and there are those who like to dwell somewhat excessively on them—Wagner was a genius of the highest order. He was fully aware of the fact and no false modesty prevented him from saying so. "I feel as the Good Lord did after the Creation," he wrote to Mathilde Wesendonk in June 1859, upon completing *Tristan*, "when he saw that it was good." It had been an intensely fruitful period. But too often we forget that genius, too, is not genius all the time, and no matter how Wagner surrounded himself with silken dressing gowns and sumptuous draperies for associative

SOURCE: Richard Wagner, *My Life* (New York: Dodd, Mead & Co., 1911).

reasons, the progress of the *Ring* was lengthy and laborious. The critical test came when the prose sketch was finished and Wagner was about to face the orchestration of the gigantic trilogy. What a task! Had he perhaps in the seven fallow years lost his musical mastery? The periods in which an artist has to live on faith, hope, and memory are often underestimated. Moreover, he was beset by every possible kind of tribulation and another year went by till, during an Italian journey in September 1853, the beginning of *Rheingold* presented itself to him. Worn out by sea-sickness, he fell into one of those threshold states between sleep and waking that provide, it would seem, the ideal condition for initiating the creative process. Is there a correlation between that intermediary state and the mysterious bare fifth of the beginning of *Rheingold?* Since the lack of the third prevents the ear from assessing mode or key, we find ourselves in a world of being not yet determined, not yet in relation. From this foggy, uncertain mystique of the primordial womb emerges the vast structure of the monumental work; in a way one may even say that it contains in germ all that follows:

> After a night spent in fever and sleeplessness, I forced myself to take a long tramp the next day through the hilly country, which was covered with pine woods. It all looked dreary and desolate, and I could not think what I should do there. Returning in the afternoon, I stretched myself, dead tired, on a hard couch, awaiting the long desired hour of sleep. It did not come; but I fell into a kind of somnolent state, in which I suddenly felt as though I were sinking in swiftly flowing water. The rushing sound formed itself in my brain into a musical sound, the chord of E-flat major, which continually reechoed in broken

forms; these broken chords seemed to be melodic passages of increasing motion, yet the pure triad of E-flat major never changed, but seemed by its continuance to impart infinite significance to the element in which I was sinking. I awoke in sudden terror from my doze, feeling as though the waves were rushing high above my head. I at once recognized that the orchestral overture to the *Rheingold*, which must long have lain latent within me, though it had been unable to find definite form, had at last been revealed to me. I then quickly realized my own nature; the stream of life was not to flow to me from without, but from within.

It was clearly a process of "reculer pour mieux sauter." From this plunge into the substratum of experience, symbolized by the magma of flowing water, Wagner returned refreshed and regenerated. Mythology abounds in such symbols, Jung's archetypes, "the psychic residue of numberless experiences of the same type," which are implanted in the memory of the race. Among these are the days and seasons, feasts and reoccurring events that have happened rhythmically throughout history. They become the trigger actions which all of a sudden assume unexpected significance by releasing the creative impulse from trivial occupations.

On Good Friday (April 10th, 1857) I awoke to find the sun shining brightly for the first time in the house: the little garden was radiant with green, the birds sang, and at last I could sit on the roof and enjoy the long-yearned-for peace with its message of promise. Full of this sentiment, I suddenly remembered that the day was Good Friday, and I called to mind the significance this omen had already once assumed for me when I was reading Wolfram's *Parzifal*. Since the sojourn in Marienbad, where

I had conceived the *Meistersinger* and *Lohengrin*, I had never occupied myself again with the poem; now its noble possibilities struck me with overwhelming force, and out of my thoughts about Good Friday I rapidly conceived a whole drama, of which I made a rough sketch with a few dashes of the pen, dividing the whole into three acts.

PARMENIDES

(c. 515 B.C.)

Being has been the central and dominating issue of Western philosophy for twenty-five hundred years and Parmenides was the great point of departure. What has been left of his work is only fragmentary; some hundred and thirty verses of epic hexameters have been preserved. And yet the impact is total and overwhelming. Here was a thinker who spoke with the voice of a visionary, with absolute self-certainty, compelled by the force of his unprecedented insight. Although the form is that of prophetic revelation, Parmenides remains a philosopher, a "knowing man": "Judge by reasoning," he admonishes, "the much-debated proofs I utter."

SOURCE: *Philosophers Speak for Themselves. From Thales to Plato.* Edited by T. V. Smith. (Chicago: University of Chicago Press, 1934).

In the introduction to his only poem, *On Nature*, Parmenides describes the philosophic journey to the heavens: as a young poet he mounts the chariot of the sun maidens, who drive him from night to daylight so swiftly, that the axle "gave forth a pipe-like sound." At the boundary between night and day, he passes through a gate that Dikē opens for him, and he is led into the presence of the goddess from whose lips he receives the truth:

> And now you must study all things: Not only the un-shaken heart of well-rounded truth but also the mortals' opinions, in which there is no true reliance . . .

Thus the poem by the command of the goddess, falls into two parts. Since our concern is with Parmenides's insight into being, the fundamental idea, contained in the first part, is this:

> Come now and I will tell thee—and do thou hear my word and heed it—what are the only ways of enquiry that lead to knowledge. The one way assuming that being is and that it is impossible for it not to be, is the trustworthy path, for truth attends it. The other, that not-being is and that it necessarily is, I call a wholly incredible course, since thou canst not recognize not-being (for this is im-possible), nor couldst thou speak of it, for thought and being are the same thing.

> It makes no difference to me at what point I begin, for I shall always come back again to this.

> It is necessary both to say and to think that being is; for it is possible that being is, and it is impossible that not-being is; this is what I bid thee ponder. I restrain thee from this first course of investigation; and from that course also along which mortals knowing nothing wander

aimlessly . . . There is left but this single path to tell thee of: Namely, that being IS.

For the first time in the history of the West a thinker expresses his surprise, his wonder, his jubilant certainty that being is. It must have been an overpowering moment, perhaps comparable to the joy men have experienced when they first became aware of tonality in music. In thanksgiving for the revelation Parmenides built a temple to the Pythagorean Ameinias, for through him he had found peace in the knowledge of the actuality of being.

Through reflection Parmenides became aware of what this being is: It is one, without origin or end, homogeneous and indivisible, immovable and unchangeable, full and spherical. Furthermore he notes that certainty of being has its origin in thinking: Hence, "thinking and that by reason of which thought exists are one and the same thing." What he had in mind was not the thinking of common sense, but authentic thinking (in the *nous*) with insight into the ground of things. In this manner of thought being is present as a whole.

It was an idea, that, in its bold simplicity, was to have an incalculable effect on the human mind. Thought had come into its own as an independent power. Later philosophers filled in the lines, defined and shaded, and two thousand years after the event such thinking became known as ontology. Parmenides remained the inexhaustible source. He was greatly admired by Plato, who, in the *Theatetus*, created a beautiful monument to him: "Parmenides is in my eyes, as Homer says, a 'revered and awe inspiring figure.' I thought there was a kind of depth in him that was altogether noble. I am afraid we might not understand his words and still less the thought they express." Nietzsche, on the other hand, believed he understood him, and

did not. To him he appeared to be the type of prophet made
not of fire but of ice. "Henceforth," he says, truth would
reside "only in the palest, most abstract generalities, in the
empty husks of the vaguest words, as in a house of spider-
webs." The nervous vibrato of Irrational Man. The not-being,
or nothingness, which Parmenides had declared to be incon-
ceivable and hence not real, suddenly yawned like a chasm
beneath the feet of post-modern man.

ANSELM OF CANTERBURY

(*1033–1109*)

One is hard put to decide what one admires most in Anselm: his soaring faith, his fearless defense of Church rights, or his uniquely penetrating intelligence. I suppose it was the intimate fusion between faith and intelligence that made him so incomparable. Coming in the first phase of the controversy on Universals, he had to meet the Nominalism of Roscelin. It was a time of fierce intellectual activity and although the edifice of the Church stood unchallenged, everything else was being vigorously questioned.

The question which Anselm asked himself was this: Can pure thought—unclouded by folly and uninfluenced by the

source: Eadmer, *Life of St. Anselm*. Edited by R. W. Southern. (New York and London: Thomas Nelson, 1962).

obedience of faith—acquire certainty of God's being? He knew the traditional proofs and used them, but they didn't suffice him. At last the solution came to him after a long period of inner struggle.

> Although I often and earnestly directed my thought to this, and at some times that which I sought seemed to be just within my reach, while again it wholly evaded my mental vision, at last in despair I was about to cease, as if from the search for a thing which could not be found. But when I wished to exclude this thought altogether . . . then more and more, though I was unwilling and shunned it, it began to force itself upon me, with a kind of importunity. So, one day when I was exceedingly wearied with resisting its importunity, in the very conflict of my thoughts, the proof of which I had despaired offered itself, so that I eagerly embraced the thoughts which I was strenuously repelling.

Anselm's biographer, Eadmer, writes:

> This thought allowed him neither to sleep, eat, nor drink and, what troubled him still more, it interfered with his devotions at matins and at other times. He believed that such thoughts might be temptations of the Devil and endeavored to banish them from his mind entirely. But the more violently he sought to do so, the more they besieged him. And one night, as he lay awake, it happened: God's grace illumined his heart, the object of his quest lay bared to his understanding, and his whole innermost being was filled with boundless rejoicing.

Enraptured by thought as thought, he found the fundamental idea, known as the ontological proof, to which he clung all his life. Starting from the notion that God is "a being than which nothing greater can be conceived," he argues that what exists in reality is greater than that which is only in the mind; hence, as God is "a being than which nothing greater can be conceived," He exists in reality. Or, to put it another way: It is so true that that which no greater can be conceived really exists, that its non-existence isn't even conceivable. The validity of this argument rests on the distinction between authentic thinking and empty discourse. "For in one sense an object is conceived when the word signifying it is conceived; and in another, when the very entity, which the object is, is understood." If I think authentically, with insight, that God is, I cannot think that God is not; but as a logical proposition the "proof" remains empty.

Anselm's great moment of inspiration was an operation of *nous* rather than *dianoia*—there was a flash, and he now knew. Eadmer, his chronicler, tells how, filled with joy, Anselm quickly wrote down his thoughts. The waxen tablets were put in the charge of one of the monks who promptly mislaid them. Anselm managed to recall the argument, wrote it down again, and put it in safer keeping. But when he needed it, he found that the wax was broken. With some difficulty he put the fragments together and had the whole copied on parchment for greater durability (this time taking no chances).

Well, one needn't be a medievalist to interpret the incident symbolically. The famous ontological proof was lost and found again, pulled to pieces and restored in the course of the centuries. Rejected by Aquinas, it was revived by Descartes, assailed by Kant, defended by Hegel, and because the substance of its thinking is eternal and ahistorical, is still with us today.

NICHOLAS OF CUSA

(1401–1464)

The Roman Church of S. Pietro in Vincoli sees an impressive throng of visitors every day of the year. They are generally conducted by a guide who steers them straight to Michelangelo's Moses. Barely anyone turns left at the entrance where the tomb of Nicholas with a delightful portrait engraving by Andrea Bregno can be found.

Nicholas Krebs was born in Kues, on the Moselle, and he came to be known as Cusanus after Cusa, the latinized form of his birthplace. He was the only one of the great philosophers who led a busy life in the world from his earliest youth

SOURCES: Nicholas of Cusa, *Of Learned Ignorance* (London: Routledge and Kegan Paul, 1954) and *The Vision of God*. Translated by Emma Gurney Salter (New York: E. P. Dutton & Co., 1960).

to his death. He served the Church as Papal Legate, Cardinal, and Vicar General in Rome and participated in all the great movements of his day. Humanism, science, politics, and what we now would call "ecumenism," they all engaged his extraordinary energies. And yet he was never wholly caught up in any of them. His true calling lay elsewhere. And this "elsewhere" he strove to express in a highly original metaphysical vision.

The fundamental idea came to him—not in the seclusion of his cell at Tegernsee to which he always hoped to retire—but in the thick of his irenic activities. In the interest of Catholic unity he made a journey to Constantinople and brought back with him as far as Venice Emperor John VI Paleologus and the Greek Patriarch, who were to participate in a Council Pope Eugene IV had called to heal the Schism. During this memorable voyage—it lasted from November 1437 to February 1438 —an extraordinary vista must have opened before him: at last, unity in the Western Church, reunion with the East, the prospect of an entire unknown world, loftier and wider than he had imagined.

It was then, in the middle of the Adriatic, that the concepts of the "coincidence of opposites" and "learned ignorance" were bestowed upon Cusanus. Much has been made of the sumptuous setting: the Doge's galley "Bucentaur," with its scarlet hangings and brilliant decorations put up by the Venetians for Emperor and Patriarch. One would prefer, perhaps, to imagine that it was the sight of the distant horizon merging into the shoreless ocean that inspired Cusanus with his insight: that the infinite eludes all relating to the finite but nevertheless is present to our awareness. Although insight is essentially a function of inner conditions and not of outer circumstances, there is still such a thing as a propitious circumstance. But this remains, of course, conjecture. All we know is that he saw in a flash the new idea that marked his initiation into philosophy. In a letter to his old friend Cardinal Cesarini he writes:

> Take now, Reverend Father, what for long I have by divers paths of learning sought to attain. Attainment, however, was denied me until I was returning by sea from Greece, when, by what I believe was a supreme gift of the Father of Light from Whom is every perfect gift, I was led in the learning that is ignorance to grasp the incomprehensible; and thus I was able to achieve not by way of comprehension but by transcending these perennial truths that can be reached by reason. In union with Him, Who is the Truth, I have now set forth the learning that is ignorance in these books, and these can be reduced or enlarged from the same source.

And this is precisely what he did all his life. From now on his writings would represent a continual modulation and enrichment of this single insight—the need to transcend conceptual thinking by the "coincidence of opposites." This was, of course, not an entirely new idea. It appears in the Neo-Platonists and can be found in Eckhart, with whose writings Cusanus must have been familiar since his early studies at Deventer. Though not a mystic himself, he was powerfully drawn in that direction, and he must have felt that with the "coincidence of opposites" and "learned ignorance" he had now found a key to their intuitive insights. It enabled him to elucidate systematically what he had up to then suspected but was unable to substantiate:

> I give Thee thanks, my God because . . . thou hast shown me that Thou canst not be seen elsewhere than where im-

possibility meets and faces me. Thou hast inspired me
. . . to do violence to myself, because impossibility co-
incides with necessity, and I have learnt . . . The place
where Thou art found unveiled . . . This place is girt
around with the coincidence of contradictories, and this
is the Wall of Paradise wherein God abides.

The spirit of conceptual thinking guards the door,

and unless he be vanquished, the way in will not lie open.
Thus it is beyond the coincidence of contradictories that
Thou mayest be seen.

This magnificently bold symbolism is employed by Cusanus
to illuminate the boundary between finite objects accessible to
discursive reason, and the infinite, that can be touched upon
only by speculative reason. When we come up against the
domain of the infinite we must keep discursive thinking in a
state of "learned" ignorance so that a new kind of thinking
can set in: it is a disciplined speculation that goes beyond all
sensory and rational experience. Here contradictions and op-
positions as we know them in finite thinking coincide, and we
are able to attain insight into what lies beyond the "Wall."
However, once stated, the thought does not come to rest; it is
impelled to go always further, and in speculation the mind is
drawn toward an ever-receding infinite:

That which sates the intellect, or that is the end thereof,
is not that which it does not understand at all, but that
alone which it understands by not understanding. For the
intelligible which it knows does not sate it, nor the intelligible of which it is utterly ignorant, but only the intelligible which it knows to be so intelligible that it can never
be fully understood—this alone can sate it.

JEAN-JACQUES ROUSSEAU

(1712–1778)

It is a curious fact that the world has never been able to make up its mind about Rousseau's character. Was he fundamentally mean or noble? Or was he simply quarrelsome to the point of madness? "He contradicts and quarrels with all mankind," wrote Horace Walpole, "in order to obtain their admiration." Wherever he went, he carried with him a spirit of unappeasable excitability, which constantly drove him into the most humiliating and absurd situations. When he arrived at. the island of St. Pierre on the lake of Bienne in 1765, he thought that he had finally found peace and said that he would happily spend

SOURCES: J.-J. Rousseau, *The Reveries of a Solitary* (London: George Routledge & Sons, 1927) and *Les Confessions*, VII (Paris: Garnier Frères, 1891).

the rest of his days on that enraptured spot. As it turned out, that abode, too, became too hot to hold him. But while he was there, he experienced an extraordinary flash of illumination which he relates in his *Reveries:*

> When the evening approached, I descended from the summits of the island, and I went gladly to sit down on the border of the lake, on the shore, in some hidden nook: There, the sound of the waves and the agitation of the water, fixing my senses and driving every other agitation from my soul, plunged it into a delicious reverie, where the night often surprised me without my having perceived it. The flux and reflux of the water, its continuous sound, swelling at intervals, struck ceaselessly my ears and my eyes, responding to the interval movements which reverie extinguished in me, and sufficed to make me feel my existence with pleasure, without taking the trouble to think. From time to time was born a brief and weak reflection on the instability of earthly things, of which the surface of the water offered me an image; but soon the light impressions effaced themselves in the uniformity of continuous movement which rocked me, and which, without any active help from my soul, did not fail to attach me to such an extent that when summoned by the hour and the signal agreed upon, I could not tear away without an effort.

His perplexed and tortured spirit was caught up by a total absorption that blotted out everything but an intense awareness of being. "I realized," he said, "that our existence is nothing but a succession of moments perceived through the senses." This doctrine spread throughout the world and filled the vacuum caused by Voltaire's sterile skepticism and by the dry agnosticism of the Encyclopedists. Kenneth Clark observes that the Cartesian "I think therefore I am" was now replaced

1784 he took up the study of anatomy—he had to steal
y from his public duties at Weimar to attend dissecting
ons at Jena—and all of a sudden, without any warning, his
d Herder received this message:

Jena, March 27. Night . . . I have found it—not gold, nor
silver, but what gives me unspeakable joy—the os inter-
maxillare in man! I compared human and animal skulls
with Loder, found the clue, and behold, here it is! But I
beg you do not let on to anyone, for this must be secretly
treated. It should fill your heart with joy for it is like the
keystone to man, not missing but present. And how!

the age of thirty-five Goethe had discovered, by methods
n foreshadowed comparative morphology, that the hu-
jawbone contained traces of a structure similar to the
maxillary bone in apes, thus linking man structurally
his animal forbears. Why did Goethe see what eluded
ecialists? I think that for one he approached the subject
ut preconceptions. He had no system, no scientific ax to
What he did have was a knowledge, won by introspec-
f his own development, how everything in his life had
d slowly, step by step. This basic psychological law
him clairvoyant to the laws of nature. And yet he re-
d from summing up his vision into a scientific formula—
s his mystical side shied away from that.
he next ten years we see him increasingly occupied with
al studies. "The world of plants is raging in me," he
shortly before his Italian journey. And then, in 1787
a walk in Padua, he observes the palm tree lovingly, like
n heart, and suddenly, the idea begins to appear to him.

by "I feel therefore I am"; "It was an intellectual time-bomb,
which after sizzling away for almost 200 years has only just
gone off, whether to the advantage of civilization seems rather
doubtful."

Rousseau, though frequently drenched in tears—*inondé de
larmes*—was nevertheless a genius, gifted with great literary
powers. His belief in the virtue and superiority of natural man
provided the motive power for the next fifty years. In his
Confessions, he recalls the moment of crisis which made him
a man of letters, a publicist and an author. It came on the
occasion of his visit to Diderot who was in prison for his
Letters to the Blind. Rousseau read an announcement in the
Mercure de France about a question proposed by the Academy
of Dijon: "Whether the revival of Sciences and Arts has
contributed to the Purification of Morals." The question answered itself in the mind of Jean Jacques almost immediately.
Reading this article while seated under an oak tree in the woods
of Vincennes, the answer to the question came to him as a
sudden flash of illumination.

If ever anything resembled a sudden inspiration, it was
the commotion which began in me as I read this. All at
once I felt myself dazzled by a thousand sparkling lights;
crowds of vivid ideas thronged into my mind with a force
and confusion that threw me into unspeakable agitation; I
felt my head whirling in a giddiness like that of intoxication. A violent palpitation oppressed me; unable to walk
for difficulty of breathing, I sank under one of the trees of
the avenue, and passed half an hour there in such a condition of excitement that when I arose I saw that the front
of my waistcoat was all wet with tears, though I was
wholly unconscious of shedding them. Ah, if ever I could
have written a quarter of what I saw and felt under that

tree, with what clearness should I have brought out all the
contradictions of our social system; with what simplicity
I should have demonstrated that man is good naturally,
and that by institutions only is he debased.

JOHANN WOLFGANG

Unlike Vasco da Gama or Columbus,
to discover, he saw and he discovere
sharper eye than he: it reached bey
plants, animals, rocks, and light. His s
him that the single individual was par
whole, and to this he surrendered hin
trust. Sometimes he carried this trust i
friends warned of drinking a glass of
it was swarming with insects, Goethe
that the small organisms would do
nourish him.

SOURCE: Emil Ludwig, *Geschichte eines Me*
Verlag, 1931).

In
awa
sessi
frier

At
whic
man
interr
with
the s
witho
grind
tion,
evolve
made
fraine
perhap
In t
botani
writes
taking
a huma

I find myself extremely close to the secret of plant creation which is the simplest thing that can be thought. The
archetypal plant will be the strangest growth the world
has ever seen, and nature herself shall envy me for it. With
such a model, and with the key to it in one's hands, one
will be able to contrive an infinite variety of plants. They
will be strictly logical plants,—in other words, even though
they may not actually exist, they could exist.

Goethe made his own botanical drawings to show that the
archetype plan of the vegetable world consisted in a number
of typical leaf forms, from which all plant structures could
be derived, apart from the stem. The first leaves which emerged
from the seed were simple in form but successive ones differ-
entiated and became more complex, developing a central rib,
indented edges, and so on. Finally, flowers and fruit organs
appeared, the petals of flowers and the parts of the fruit organs, being, according to Goethe, merely modified leaves.

This discovery, like so many great insights, was very simple:
by tracing the manifold shapes of plants from one fundamental
type, he had established their evolutionary development. Ten
years later he called these days the happiest of his life.

From the realm of plants it was only one step to that of
animals. One day, at the Jewish cemetery in Venice, his servant laughingly presented him with what he believed to be a
human skull. But Goethe identified it as a split ram's skull,
and, recalling his discovery a decade ago of the intermaxillary
bone, he saw what nobody else had seen: that the skull did not
consist of planes of bone but of vertebrae. From this he con-
cluded that every bone was essentially a part or fragment of a
vertebra. Thus he became the first to lay down a leading concept of comparative anatomy. More important still, he stated

that "a common type, striving for evolutionary development (metamorphosis) goes through all organic life, can be observed at certain intermediary stages, and must also be acknowledged when, at the highest human stage, it modestly retreats into hiddenness." Seen through the loving eyes of the poet, nature led to living nature, law to form. This insight anticipated the ideas of organic evolution seventy years before Charles Darwin.

CHARLES DARWIN

(1809–1882)

As we have seen, evolution, the theory that all species evolve from a common ancestor, was by no means new. Charles Darwin's grandfather, Erasmus, had arrived at a formulation similar to Goethe's, and Lamarck provided the first logical theory in which he attributed evolution to the cumulative inheritance of modifications induced by environment. Together with Saint-Hilaire and Robert Chambers they paved the way for Darwin's theory of natural selection, which, when it came, shook the nineteenth century like a revolution.

Frequently, great discoveries consist of clusters of insights which in retrospect appear telescoped into one. In Darwin's

SOURCE: Charles Darwin, *The Origin of the Species* (London: J. Murray, 6th ed., 1873).

case we can distinguish two, separated by more than a year. How did they come about?

What first had excited the early evolutionists, that "species had not been independently created, but had descended, like varieties, from other species," had ended for Darwin in a cul de sac. It gave no satisfactory explanation of the reasons which caused the common ancestor to transform itself gradually, and thus the hypothesis remained for him an empty tautology. At this point Darwin must have felt all the heavens press down on him, similar to Archimedes before he took to his bath. Without this pressure he would have failed to make the observation that ended the deadlock: that the world of animal breeding could be linked to the descent of man.

> It seemed to me probable that a careful study of domesticated animals and of cultivated plants would offer the best chance of making out this complicated problem. Nor have I been disappointed; in this and in other perplexing cases I have invariably found that our knowledge, imperfect though it be, of variation under domestication, afforded the best and safest clue. I may venture to express the conviction of the high value of such studies, although they have been very commonly neglected by naturalists.

The discovery of evolution through selection was, however, only the first phase. New difficulties began to appear almost immediately. In controlled experiments it was obviously man who was the agent of selection. But what about wild animals and plants? "How selection could be applied to organisms living in a state of nature remained for some time a mystery to me." This time the problem was even more tantalizing and for a whole year Darwin tried to bypass the difficulty, but to no avail. It was a genuine impasse. Then he came upon Thomas

Malthus's *Essay On The Principle Of Population* in which is developed the theory that the human race tends to outrun its means of sustenance and hence can be kept within bounds only by famine and other catastrophes. This showed Darwin the concept he was looking for.

> In October 1838, I happened to read for amusement Malthus on population, and being well prepared to appreciate the struggle for existence which everywhere goes on, from long continued observation of the habits of animals and plants, it at once struck one that under these circumstances favorable variations would tend to be preserved, and unfavorable ones destroyed. The result of this would be the formation of a new species. Here then I had a theory by which to work.

The fact that the work of that depressing clergyman should fall into Darwin's hands forty years after it was written is, of course, mere chance. But the genius takes what he needs. Had he not seen the book, other factors, no doubt, would have presented themselves to his inquiring mind. Now that the theory was complete, the rest was merely a question of elaboration.

Curiously enough, Darwin's friend A. R. Wallace went through a similar process.

Wallace was lying ill with intermittent fever at Ternate in February 1858 when he began to think of Malthus' *Essay on Population*, read several years before: suddenly the idea of the survival of the fittest flashed upon him. In two hours he had "thought out almost the whole theory," and in three evenings had finished his essay.*

* *Encyclopaedia Britannica*, VII (13th edition).

Here the work of Malthus did not spontaneously cause the insight but was stored in the subconscious till, at the propitious moment it emerged in full clarity. Darwin had not yet published the *Origin of Species* and the two scientists submitted their works jointly to the Linean Society. The effect can be likened to that of a bomb. According to Freud, Darwin inflicted a wound upon man by making him somewhat of a chance product of seemingly blind biological forces. In the light of all that happened since the publication of Darwin's book, a prophecy has come true which Darwin himself wrote in his notebook twenty years before the publication of his *Origin of Species:* "My theory will lead to a complete new philosophy." And so it did.

PIERRE TEILHARD DE CHARDIN

(1881-1955)

Pierre Teilhard de Chardin has caught the imagination of our age, and sides are taken for and against him by many. There are those who regard him with enthusiasm for daring—with success—to reconcile the claims of modern science with those of Christianity. There are others who refuse to be stampeded and consider his attempt to harmonize scientific hypotheses with the supernatural naive. We cannot predict with any certainty what the verdict of the future will be. What is certain is that he blazed new trails and returned with a vision of extraordinary grandeur. He also added the cosmic sense to our faculties.

SOURCE: Nicholas Corte, *Pierre Teilhard de Chardin. His Life and Spirit* (New York: The Macmillan Company, 1961). Copyright © Barrie Books Ltd., 1960. Selection below reprinted by permission of the Macmillan Company and Barrie Books Ltd., London.

Born in the Auvergne, the country of Vercingetorix and of Pascal, near the plain of Clermont and the beautiful Puy mountains, he had since early childhood felt close to the earth. His "sacred objects" were drawn from nature. One should, however, beware of using the word "nature" too loosely; we are told that there are fifty-two meanings that can be attached to it. Well, it surely wasn't Rousseau's nature, nor even Blake's nor was it the daffodils of the English Romantics. I suppose Teilhard's idea of nature was most akin to Goethe's idea of metamorphosis, a gradual evolving and striving for further development. For him nature also meant scientific research— which he later on declared to be a third dimension, a third infinity in our universe, along with the infinitely small and the infinitely great.

In a manuscript entitled "The Heart of the Matter," Teilhard, now near the end of his life, traces the source of his illuminating idea to childhood. What he sees most clearly is a double appeal, from God and from Matter. There is a subdued exhilaration in those passages, and a strong sense of mission, and the single-mindedness of genius.

> However far I go back in my childhood, the most characteristic and the most familiar thing I find in my inner attitude is the yearning or irresistible need for some "*one thing sufficient and necessary*." To be completely at ease, to be entirely happy I needed to know that "*some one essential thing*" existed, to which everything else was only accessory or even an ornament. I needed to know it, and to be able to play endlessly with the consciousness of this existence. Indeed, if as I look back I am able to recognize myself at all and to follow my path, it is only by the trace of this note, this tinge, or this particular flavour in my life. And this is something which, however little of it one

has once experienced, it is impossible to mistake for any other of the passions of the soul—neither the joy of knowledge nor that of discovery nor that of creating nor of loving; not so much because it is different from all of them, but because it is of a high order and contains all of them . . .

I was certainly no more than six or seven when I began to feel myself drawn by Matter—or more exactly by something that "shone" at the heart of Matter. At this age when I suppose other children feel their first "sentiment" for a person or for art or for religion, I was affectionate, well-behaved, even pious. That is, catching it from my mother, I loved "the little Lord Jesus" dearly. But in reality my genuine self was quite elsewhere. To find out about this you would have had to watch me as I withdrew, always secretly and without a word, without even thinking that there was anything worth saying about it to anyone, to contemplate, indeed to possess, to savour the existence of my "God, Iron." Yes, just that: Iron. I can still see with extraordinary clarity the whole series of my "idols." In the country a plough-key which I hid away carefully in a corner of the courtyard. In town, the hexagonal head of a metal staple which stuck out at the level of the nursery floor and which I took possession of . . .

I can't help smiling today when I think of these pranks. Yet at the same time I am forced to recognize that in this instinctive movement which made me truly speaking *Worship* a little piece of metal, there was a strong sense of self-giving and a whole train of obligations all mixed up together; and my whole spiritual life has merely been the development of this.

In another passage of the same book he describes the course of his scientific curiosity. It had first been kindled by geology, all around it was, almost incidentally, the growing appeal of vegetable and animal Nature; and deeper down, one fine day, came my initiation into the less tangible, but no less tempting, grandeurs revealed by the researches of physics. On each side of Matter stood Life and Energy: the three pillars of my inward vision and happiness.

But the fundamental insight, the totality of his vision is present from the first. There are no breaks and reversals. At this time too, the idea of evolution begins to develop, "like a seed sprung from I don't know where."

> I remember clearly having read [Bergson's] *Creative Evolution* with avidity at this time. But although I didn't very well understand at this period what exactly Bergson's Durée meant—and in any case it was not sufficiently convergent to satisfy me—I can see clearly that the effect of these passionate pages on me was merely, at the right moment and in a flash, to stir up a fire that was already burning in my heart and mind.

Evolution, for him, meant something much more momentous than Darwin's transformation of the species—which took no account of the spirit of man. It was a continuous movement on a cosmic scale, under the pressure of the Creator, with man not the centre, but the axis and apex of the Universe. This august conception was "a magic key that kept coming back to my mind, like a refrain, or a taste, a promise and an appeal:"

> During my years of theology at Hastings, that is just after experiencing the marvels of Egypt, little by little I grew more and more conscious, less as an abstract notion than

as a presence, of a profound, ontological total drift of the Universe around me: so conscious of this that it filled my whole horizon.

The magnetic needle of his spirit pointed towards this pole and never wavered from it.

JOHN STUART MILL

(1806–1873)

"Madmen in authority," wrote the late Lord Keynes, "who hear voices in the air, are distilling their frenzy from some academic scribbler of a few years back." John Stuart Mill was such a "scribbler," a man of extraordinary stature, and by universal consent, the greatest economist of his age. Like other eminent Victorians he combined intellectual distinction with a very admirable character. His upbringing is a shattering refutation of laissez-faire educational theories: at the age of three he read Greek, and by the time he had reached eight, he had mastered a formidable amount of classical, historical, and ec-

sources: John Stuart Mill, *Autobiography* (New York: Columbia University Press, 1924) and *Principles of Political Economy* (New York: Longmans, Green & Co., 1909).

clesiastical history. Between eight and twelve he galloped through algebra, geometry, and differential calculus, wrote several histories, and even some poetry. And at thirteen, he studied all there was to be known about political economy.

There followed, of course, a crisis. The event is movingly described in Mill's *Autobiography:*

> It was in the autumn of 1826. I was in a dull state of nerves, such as everybody is occasionally liable to; unsusceptible to enjoyment or pleasurable excitement; one of those moods when what is pleasure at other times, becomes insipid or indifferent; the state, I should think, in which converts to Methodism usually are, when smitten by their first "conviction of sin." In this frame of mind it occurred to me to put the question directly to myself: "Suppose that all your objects in life were realized; that all the changes in institutions and opinions which you are looking forward to, could be completely effected at this very instant: would this be a great joy and happiness to you?" And an irrepressible self-consciousness distinctly answered, "No!" At this my heart sank within me: the whole foundation on which my life was constructed fell down. All my happiness was to have been found in the continual pursuit of this end. The end had ceased to charm, and how could there ever again be any interest in the means? I seemed to have nothing left to live for.
>
> In all probability my case was by no means so peculiar as I fancied it, and I doubt not that many others have passed through a similar state; but the idiosyncrasies of my education had given to the general phenomenon a special character, which made it seem the natural effect of causes that it was hardly possible for time to remove. I frequently asked myself, if I could, or if I was bound to go on living, when life must be passed in this manner. I gen-

erally answered to myself, that I did not think I could possibly bear it beyond a year. When, however, not more than half that duration of time had elapsed, a small ray of light broke in upon my gloom. I was reading, accidentally, Marmontel's *Memoires,* and came to the passage which relates his father's death, the distressed position of the family, and the sudden inspiration by which he, then a mere a boy, felt and made them feel that he would be everything to them—would supply the place of all that they had lost. A vivid conception of the scene and its feelings came over me, and I was moved to tears. From this moment my burden grew lighter. The oppression of the thought that all feeling was dead within me, was gone. I was no longer hopeless: I was not a stock or a stone. I had still, it seemed, some of the material out of which all worth of character, and all capacity for happiness, was made. Relieved from my ever present sense of irremediable wretchedness, I gradually found that the ordinary incidents of life could again give me some pleasure; that I could again find some enjoyment, not intense, but sufficient for cheerfulness, in sunshine and sky, in books, in conversation, in public affairs; and that there was, once more, excitement, though of a moderate kind, in exerting myself for my opinions, and for the public good.

A Freudian generation may interpret the incident differently, but, whatever its causes, the attack of accidie turned out to be a blessing in disguise. Reading Wordsworth, Goethe, and Saint-Simon helped him to blend the harshness of his earlier life with a touch of the Romantic movement. And finally there was the "incomparable friend," Mrs. Taylor, to whose influence Mill attributed almost too generously the entire body of his work.

At the age of forty-three Mill wrote his magnum opus of

economics, the two splendidly written volumes of the *Principles of Political Economy*. In reviewing his subject as a static science, Mill's ideas are derived from his orthodox predecessors with only minor modifications. The laws that governed production were hard facts received up to our own day as commonplaces. When, however, he turned from the static to the dynamic aspect of economy, he became truly original. Here lay the domain of his great insight: the proper province of economic law was distribution and not production:

> The things once there, mankind, individually or collectively, can do with them as they please. They can place them at the disposal of whomsoever they please, and on whatever terms . . . Even what a person has produced by his individual toil, unaided by anyone, he cannot keep, unless by the permission of society. Not only can society take it from him, but individuals could and would take it from him, if society . . . did not . . . employ and pay people for the purpose of preventing him from being disturbed in (his) possession. The distribution of wealth, therefore, depends on the laws and customs of society. The rules by which it is determined are what the opinions and feeling of the ruling portion of the community make them, and are very different in different ages and countries, and might be still more different, if mankind so chose . . .

Economics, then, depend on society, not society on economics. The absolute rules that had been regarded as inevitable as bad weather were not absolute at all but manmade and, thus, variable from one civilization or age to another. This was a discovery of tremendous importance. "It lifted," writes Professor Heilbroner, "the whole economic debate from the stifling realm of impersonal and inevitable law and brought it back into the arena of ethics and morality. After Mill, economists might argue that men *deserved* such and such remuneration for this or that reason, but they could never again pretend that some abstract arithmetical force *decreed* that this was the way it should be done."

Like all great insights, once uttered, they become incredibly simple and obvious. Moreover, they pass into the habitual texture of our minds so that after a while the most revolutionary discoveries seem commonplace, and we marvel less at the discovery than at our own obtuseness which prevented us from seeing what was there all the time.

WILLIAM HARVEY

(1578–1657)

William Harvey, celebrated physician and anatomist, was born in Kent when Shakespeare was fourteen years old. His face resembles Shakespeare's but in his expression are traces of tension and aloofness. Except for his King, Charles I, he had few friends, and outside of drinking coffee and reading Virgil he had few pleasures. He liked walking in the fields and sitting in the dark, thinking. What he thought led to perhaps the most important medical discovery ever made: The circulation of the blood.

The traditional view, held since late antiquity and the Middle Ages, that there were three different physiological fluids in

SOURCE: William Harvey, *Works*. Translated by R. Willis. (London: The Sydenham Society, 1847 and New York: Johnson Reprint Corp., 1965).

the human body, two being different kinds of blood, had been a great obstacle in the development of a circulatory theory. At the beginning of the seventeenth century the prevalent view was that the blood moved back and forth in the veins and arteries like a tide. When that concept was finally destroyed, the way to the new theory lay open. And yet no one arrived at a finished doctrine before Harvey, though men like Servetus, Cesalpino, and Giordano Bruno had been speculating about the idea. It took perhaps the scientific revolution to give the heart and the blood that primacy of place which the Sun held in the new system. Harvey wrote:

> The heart is the beginning of life; the Sun of the microcosm, even as the Sun in his turn might well be designated the heart of the world; for it is the heart by whose virtue and pulse the blood is moved, perfected, made apt to nourish, and is preserved from corruption and coagulation; it is the household divinity which, discharging its function, nourishes, cherishes, quickens the whole body, and is indeed the foundation of life, the source of all action . . . The heart, like the prince in a kingdom, in whose hands lie the chief and highest authority, rules over all; it is the original and foundation from which all power is derived, on which all power depends in the animal body.

It was the absolutist view which inspired this panegyric and which now began to replace the hierarchical one of the Middle Ages. Curiously enough, Harvey found in Aristotle the analogy that proved to be the clue for his insight: the circular motion within the terrestrial sphere is somewhat akin to the circular motion of the blood, since man was considered the microcosm of the whole world:

I began to think whether there might not be a motion as it were in a circle, in the same way as Aristotle says that the air and the rain emulate the circular motion of the superior bodies: for the moist earth warmed by the sun evaporates; the vapours drawn upwards are condensed, and descending in the form of rain moistening the earth again; and by this arrangement are generations of living things produced; and in like manner too are tempests and meteors engendered by their circular motion, and by the approach and recession of the Sun. And so in all likelihood does it come to pass in the body, through the motion of the blood.

It was this initial flash, connecting the hitherto unconnected, that put Harvey on the track of the circulatory theory. He now sought to verify his idea empirically and he found solid evidence for it. It became first known in a lecture delivered at the Royal College of Physicians in 1616 and the notes he made in a hurried and almost illegible hand, miraculously survived:

W. H. Constat perfabricam cordis sanguinem per pulmones in aorta perpetua transferri, as two clacks of a water bellows to rays water constat per ligaturam transitium sanguinis . . .*

Here was the first written mention of the theory of the circulation of the blood. Although Harvey lived to see the truth of his discovery widely acknowledged, it remained for others to exploit the practical side of his great insight.

* It is proved by the structure of the heart that the blood is continually transferred through the lungs into the aorta as by two clacks of a water bellows to raise water. It is proved by the ligature that there is a perpetual flow of blood . . ." (Translated by Agatha Young.)

WILHELM CONRAD RÖNTGEN

(1845–1923)

Wilhelm Conrad Röntgen, the discoverer of x-rays, is an immensely impressive figure. He possessed high ability as a theorist, genius for experimentation, and that nobility of outlook which made him refuse any financial gain that might have accrued from an exploitation of his discovery. He was a university professor, a scientist, a benefactor of mankind. Here was glory enough. To this idealistic code he adhered all his life, and when in 1901, the year of its inception, he was awarded the Nobel Prize for his contribution to physics, he left the 50,000 Swedish crowns to the University of Würzburg to be used in the interest of science. "Compared to the inner satis-

source: Otto Glasser, *Dr. W. C. Röntgen* (Springfield, Ill.: Charles C Thomas, 1968). Selection below reprinted by permission of Charles C Thomas, Publisher.

faction derived from a successfully solved problem," he said after the conferring of honors, "all exterior appreciation loses its significance."

This interior satisfaction he must have experienced most keenly during his fiftieth year. For several months he had found himself captivated by the work of Crookes and Lenard with cathode rays. In studying the real properties of this flow of charged particles which Crookes had called a new "fourth state of matter," Lenard had observed that they produced luminescent effects on certain salts and a darkening effect on photographic plate. By repeating Lenard's experiments, on November 8, 1895 Röntgen discovered that a surprising thing happened when cathode rays smashed into solid matter.

> Late one afternoon when, as was his custom and preference, he was working alone in the laboratory, he determined to test the ability of a Hittorf-Crookes tube, that is, an all glass tube without a thin window, to produce fluorescence on the barium platino-cyanide screen. Selecting a pear-shaped tube from the rack, he covered it with pieces of black cardboard, carefully cut and pasted together to make a jacket similar to the one used previously on the Lenard tube, and then hooked the tube onto the electrodes of the Ruhmkorff coil. After darkening the room in order to test the opacity of the black paper cover, he started the induction coil and passed a high tension discharge through the tube. To his satisfaction no light penetrated the cardboard cover.
>
> He was prepared to interrupt the current to set up the screen for the crucial experiment when suddenly, about a yard from the tube, he saw a weak light that shimmered on a little bench he knew was located nearby. It was as though a ray of light or faint spark from the induction

coil had been reflected by a mirror. Not believing this possible, he passed another series of discharges through the tube, and again the same fluorescence appeared, this time looking like faint green clouds moving in unison with the fluctuating discharges of the coil. Highly excited, Röntgen lit a match and to his great surprise discovered that the source of the mysterious light was the little barium platinocyanide screen lying on the bench. He repeated the experiment again and again, each time moving the little screen farther away from the tube and each time getting the same result. There seemed to be only one explanation for the phenomenon. Evidently something emanated from the Hittorf-Crookes tube that produced an effect upon the fluorescent screen at a much greater distance than he had ever observed in his Cathode ray experiments, even when he had used Lenard tubes with the thin aluminum windows.

Realizing that this conclusion was certainly in contradiction to general knowledge about Cathode rays and especially his own experience that Cathode rays never penetrated more than a few centimeters of air, he became deeply absorbed in attempting to explain the strange phenomenon. His concentration was so intense that he was completely unaware of the passage of time and of his surroundings. Marstaller, the diener of the institute, knocked on the door, entered the laboratory to look for a piece of apparatus, and left without being noticed. As the evening hours wore on, Röntgen's excitement in the peculiar inexplicable observation increased. Several times Mrs. Röntgen sent a servant to call him for dinner, and when he finally sat down to the table, he ate little and in almost complete silence. The meal was hardly finished before he returned to the laboratory. He had made no reply when Mrs. Röntgen asked him what was the matter, and his return to the laboratory in a state of suppressed excitement she ascribed to a fit of bad humor . . .

If the emanation could penetrate air to a hitherto unobserved degree, it was possible that it could also penetrate other substances. The inspiration came to him because of a peculiar shadow on the green fluorescent screen, apparently caused by a wire running across the tube from an induction coil. To test the truth of the conjecture he held a piece of paper, then a playing card, and then a book between the tube and the screen and closed the switch to the inductor. Simultaneously with the passage of the current through the tube the little screen behind the paper and the book lit up; the fluorescence for the book was not quite so bright as before, but it was certainly distinctly visible. He then collected some other materials, sheets of various metals, and placing them between the tube and the screen, he found that a thin aluminum sheet affected the fluorescence to approximately the same degree as had the book, but that a thin sheet of lead seemed to stop the rays completely. Already he was thinking of the new agent in terms of rays, since it had a few properties in common with known radiation, such as traveling in straight lines from the focus and throwing regular shadows. To test further the ability of lead to stop the rays, he selected a small lead piece, and in bringing it into position observed to his amazement not only that the round dark shadow of the disk appeared on the screen, but that he suddenly could distinguish the outline of his thumb and finger, within which appeared darker shadows—the bones of his hands.

Röntgen has told us of the exultation he felt during that memorable night. He found his feelings summarized in the words of the great engineer Werner von Siemens:

If some phenomenon that has been shrouded in obscurity suddenly emerges into the light of knowledge, if the key of a long sought mechanical combination has been found, if the missing link of a chain of thought is fortuitously supplied, this then gives the discoverer the exultant feeling that comes with a victory of the mind, which alone can compensate him for all the struggle and effort, and lift him to a higher plane of existence.

On this higher plane Röntgen lived during the following weeks. He ate and slept in the laboratory carrying out his experiments in full secrecy. It was necessary to base his findings on sound experimentation before they could be presented to the public. Then, after seven weeks, on December 28, 1895, a manuscript that bore the modest title *On a New Kind of Rays*, a preliminary communication, was presented to the Würzburg Physical-Medical Society. It is a masterful representation of the wonderful properties of the newly discovered phenomenon. "For the sake of brevity," it says in the paper, "I should like to use the term 'rays,' and to distinguish them from others, I shall use the name 'x-rays.' " Within a few weeks Röntgen found himself the center of international praise and enthusiasm. It was a sensational event. Although accidental x-ray photos had been taken by Crookes and Goodspeed before, the phenomenon had remained largely unexplained. Sir William Crookes, the inventor of the vacuum tube that bears his name, had noticed as early as 1879 that photographic plates which had been lying about during his experiments, had shown cloudy spots. Failing to grasp the relation between the tube and the plates, he returned them to the manufacturer with the complaint that they were badly fogged. He had missed the initial clue. Röntgen alone grasped the significance of an apparently unimportant effect and traced it to its proper cause. There were, of course, those who attributed his discovery to mere chance. Münsterberg, the Harvard philosopher, silenced their objections:

> Suppose chance helped. There were many Galvanic effects in the world before Galvani saw by chance the contraction of a frog's leg on an iron gate. The world is always full of such chance, and only the Galvanis and Röntgens are few.

There is indeed a correlation between merit and chance, native endowment and external circumstances. Yet with insight the internal conditions are paramount. It could not have emerged without a habitual orientation of the mind, a constant alertness that never tires of asking the little question—why?

JAMES D. WATSON

(1928–   )

We are told that Archimedes was so delighted with his discovery that he jumped out of his bath and ran naked through
the streets of Syracuse uttering the cryptic cry "Eureka." James
Watson and Francis Crick rushed from the Cavendish Laboratory in Cambridge to a pub, the Eagle, to announce exultantly
that they had discovered the secret of life. And in a way they
had. For the unravelling of the incredibly complex and
aesthetically perfect structure of DNA (deoxyribonucleic acid)
was a scientific event of the highest order: Here was the key
to the master molecule of life in which lay hidden the mys-

SOURCE: J. D. Watson, *The Double Helix* (New York: Atheneum, 1968).
© 1968 by James D. Watson. Selection below reprinted by permission of Atheneum Publishers and Weidenfeld and Nicholson Ltd.,
London.

teries of heredity and growth, perhaps even of memory and intelligence.

Since both Watson and Crick were not specialists in the most rigorous sense of the term, and since the final model of the extremely long and complicated DNA molecule proved to be such a smooth solution, it has been suggested by some that the discovery was made by a stroke of good luck. But if it was that easy, why had nobody before them hit upon DNA's double-helical shape? Many sat under apple trees but it took Newton to realize that the force that tugs an apple is the same force that keeps the moon from flying into space. "Science," wrote Watson in the preface to the *Double Helix*, "seldom proceeds in the straightforward, logical manner imagined by outsiders." Not all insights are invulnerable and hit the bull's eye; some are merely vulnerable, which means that there remain further questions to be asked on the same issue. Watson's "Cozy Corner Insight" seems to belong to this category. Although it was not the step that led to the final triumph, it is remarkable for its creative matchmaking that brought TMV tobacco mosiac virus) and crystals under one roof.

Conceivably a few additional x-ray pictures would tell how the protein subunits were arranged. This was particularly true if they were helically stacked. Excitedly I pilfered Bernal's and Fankucken's papers from the Philosophical Library and brought it up to the lab so that Francis could inspect the TMV x-ray picture. When he saw the blank regions that characterize helical patterns, he jumped into action, quickly spilling out several possible helical TMV structures. From this moment on, I knew I could no longer avoid actually understanding the Helical Theory. Waiting until Francis had free time to help me would save me from having to master the mathematics, but only at the penalty of my standing still if Francis was out of the room. Luckily, only a superficial grasp was needed to see why the TMV x-ray picture suggested a helix with a turn every 23A along the helical axis. The rules were, in fact, so simple that Francis considered writing them up under the title, *Fourier Transforms for the Birdwatcher*. This time, however, Francis did not carry the ball and on subsequent days maintained that the evidence for a TMV helix was only so-so. My morale automatically went down, until I hit upon a foolproof reason why subunits should be helically arranged. In a moment of after-supper boredom I had read a Faraday Society Discussion of *The Structure of Metals*. It contained an ingenious theory by the theoretician F. C. Frank on how crystals grow. Every time the calculations were properly done, the paradoxical answer emerged that the crystals could not grow at anywhere near the observed rates. Frank saw that the paradox vanished if crystals were not as regular as suspected, but contained dislocations resulting in the perpetual presence of *Cozy Corners* into which new molecules could fit.

Several days later, on the bus to Oxford, the notion came to me that each TMV particle should be thought of as a tiny crystal growing like other crystals through the possession of Cozy Corners. Most important, the simplest way to generate Cozy Corners was to have the subunits helically arranged. The idea was so simple that it had to be right. Every helical staircase I saw that weekend in Oxford made me more confident that other biological structures would also have helical symmetry. For over a week I pored over electron micrographs of muscle and collagen fibers, looking for hints of helices. Francis, however, remained lukewarm, and in the absence of any hard facts I knew it was futile to try to bring him around.

EDWARD GIBBON

(1737–1794)

"Monsieur Gibbon n'est point mon homme," said Rousseau. And he wasn't. It is difficult to imagine what the precursor of Romanticism could have had in common with the eighteenth-century English gentleman who was so decidedly his antithesis. Edward Gibbon's genius was almost entirely on the classical side—the Apollonian virtues of order, clarity, and control pervaded all. And this was precisely the combination needed to put order in the chaos of a thousand years' history. But far more, the task required an almost sublime confidence: in his age, its beliefs, and in his own powers to finish that enormous

SOURCES: Edward Gibbon, *The Autobiographies*. Edited by John Murray. (London: Murray, 1896) and *The Decline and Fall of the Roman Empire* (New York: Harcourt, Brace & Co., 1960).

monument of erudition *The Decline and Fall of the Roman Empire.*

Gibbon was followed all his life by tremendous good fortune but at one point it seemed to have forsaken him: His father could not provide the five hundred pounds necessary to send him across the Alps to complete his education as an English gentleman. Moreover, Gibbon was painfully casting about for a subject with an obvious lack of inspiration which, Professor Toynbee observes, "was reminiscent of the deplorable attitude prevalent among latter-day candidates for post-graduate degrees." However, his father finally produced the money, and on October 15, 1764, on the Capitoline Hill, outside of The Church of Ara Coeli, the impact occurred between Rome and her historian. Gibbon tells us of his moment of high inspiration in the *Autobiography:*

> My temper is not very susceptible of enthusiasm, and which I do not feel I have ever scorned to affect. But at the distance of twenty-five years I can neither forget nor express the strong emotions which agitated my mind as I first approached and entered the eternal city. After a sleepless night, I trod, with a lofty step, the ruins of the Forum; each memorable spot where Romulus stood, or Tully spoke, or Caesar fell, was at once present to my eye; and several days of intoxication were lost or enjoyed before I could descend to a cool and minute investigation . . . It was at Rome, on the 15th of October 1764, as I sat musing amidst the ruins of the Capitol, while the barefooted friars were singing vespers in the temple of Jupiter, that the idea of writing the Decline and Fall of the city first started to my mind.

When, in the final elegiac chapters of the Epilogue, he contemplates, through the eyes of Poggius, the state of sixteenth-century Rome, his thoughts must have again reverted to that October day on which he had first beheld the tragic contrast between the present ruins and their past magnificence when they stood intact:

The place and the object gave ample scope for moralising on the vicissitudes of fortune, which spares neither man nor the proudest of his works, which buries empires and cities in a common grave; and it was agreed that, in proportion to her former greatness, the fall of Rome was the more awful and deplorable. "Her primaeval state, such as she might appear in a remote age, when Evander entertained the stranger of Troy, has been delineated by the fancy of Virgil. This Tarpeian rock was then a savage and solitary thicket: in the time of the poet it was crowned with the golden roofs of a temple; the temple is overthrown, the gold has been pillaged, the wheel of fortune has accomplished her revolution, and the sacred ground is again disfigured with thorns and brambles. The hill of the Capitol, on which we sit, was formerly the head of the Roman empire, the citadel of the earth, the terror of kings; illustrated by the footsteps of so many triumphs, enriched with the spoils and tributes of so many nations. This spectacle of the world, how is it fallen! how changed! how defaced! the path of victory is obliterated by vines, and the benches of the senators are concealed by a dunghill. Cast your eyes on the Palatine hill, and seek among the shapeless and enormous fragments the marble theatre, the obelisks, the colossal statues, the porticoes of Nero's palace: survey the other hills of the city, the vacant space is interrupted only by ruins and gardens. The forum of the Roman people, where they assembled to enact their laws and elect their magistrates, is now enclosed for the cultivation of potherbs, or thrown open for the reception of swine and buffaloes. The public and private edifices, that were founded for eternity, lie prostrate, naked, and broken, like the limbs of a mighty giant; and the ruin is the more visible, from the stupendous relics that have survived the injuries of time and fortune."

The powerful flash of inspiration—the only one with which Gibbon was ever visited—took such hold upon his heart, that he commemorated it once more, twenty-three years after the event, in the gentle diminuendo of the *Decline and Fall's* final paragraph:

It was among the ruins of the Capitol that I first conceived the idea of a work which has amused and exercised near twenty years of my life, and which, however inadequate to my own wishes, I finally deliver to the curiosity and candour of the public.

ARNOLD TOYNBEE

(1889–   )

There is no historical truth which is, strictly speaking, incontestably true; every great historian begins with a theory, and though he modifies it in the face of evidence, he is nevertheless driven by it to select his facts. Whereas Gibbon attributed the fall of the Roman Empire to the triumph of religion and barbarism, Arnold Toynbee sees a failure of response to a challenge, the disaffection of the masses at a time of crisis. In his huge and sprawling *A Study of History*, the product of twenty years labor, Professor Toynbee proposes a cyclical pattern to explain the rise and fall of the twenty-odd civilizations which, by his count, have existed since man emerged

SOURCE: Arnold Toynbee, *A Study of History*, X (New York and London: Oxford University Press, 1954). Selection below reprinted by permission of Oxford University Press.

from primitive culture. He says that we can hear the beat of
an elemental rhythm "whose variations we have learnt to know
as challenge and response, withdrawal and return, rout and
rally, apparentation and affiliation, schism and palingenesis."
Such an all-embracing view of history drew heavy fire from
the "dry-as-dust" historians who prefer to look coldly at history and refuse to draw horoscopes of the future. Toynbee,
however, wants desperately to see a pattern in human experience and in order to explain his formula of challenge and
response, brings to bear an immense body of evidence from
the stores of universal history. By comparing the experiences
of societies across the ages, it occurred to him that two events,
though spaced wide apart chronologically, could be mentally
contemporaneous. He tells how the clue to this synoptic view
of history came to him on a long summer's day on the twenty-
third of May 1912, as he sat "musing on the summit of the
citadel at Mistrà," near Sparta in the Peloponnese.

> Though he had sat there, musing and gazing (and
> prosaically taking the edge off his hunger by consuming
> slabs of Pavlidhis' chocolate) through most of a summer's
> day, till the gloom of evening constrained him reluc-
> tantly at last to move on in search of supper and a bed at
> Trýpi, he cannot pretend that he was inspired during his
> reverie on the summit by any strains from the throats of
> the nuns serving the church of the Pandánassa, for he had
> left this far below in his spiral ascent of the miniature
> purgatorial mount that the citadel crowned like a Dantean
> Earthly Paradise. The sensuous experience that activated
> his historical imagination was not a sound of liturgical
> chanting; it was the sight of the ruins among which he
> had wound his way upwards to the peak; and this spec-
> tacle had been appalling; for, in this shattered fairy city,

Time had stood still since that spring of A.D. 1821 in which Mistrà had been laid desolate, in the spring of A.D. 1912 the nuns (rare birds in a Greek Orthodox Christendom) were the solitary inhabitants of a kástro that, for some six hundred years ending in the final catastrophe, had been the capital of Laconia under a series of successive régimes. Founded by the Franks circa A.D. 1249, recovered by the Byzantines in A.D. 1262, conquered by the 'Osmanlis in A.D. 1460, wrested from Ottoman hands by the Venetians in A.D. 1687, and recovered by the 'Osmanlis in A.D. 1715, Mistrà had continued, through all these political, religious, and cultural vicissitudes, to reign for those six hundred years as the queen of the broad landscape that could be surveyed from her topmost battlements; and then, one April morning, out of the blue, the avalanche of wild highlanders from the Máni had overwhelmed her; her citizens had been forced to flee for their lives and had been despoiled and massacred as they fled; her deserted mansions had been sacked; and her ruins had been left desolate from that day to this.

Gazing across the plain which stretched away from this ruined hilltown's foot to her trim and respectable lowland successor near the banks of the Eurotas where he had passed the previous night, and reading in the guidebook in his hand that "the present Sparta . . . founded in A.D. 1834 under King Otho after the War of Independence . . . is of entirely modern origin," he was convicted of a horrifying sense of the sin manifest in the conduct of human affairs. Why should this lovely medieval eyrie have to be put to the sack in order that a commonplace modern townlet might be laid out on a different site to serve the selfsame public purpose? The history of Laconia between A.D. 1821 and A.D. 1834 had been a typical sample of human history in general. (Quam parvâ sapientiâ mundus regitur)! A Gibbon might well find it difficult to decide whether Man's most damning vice was his brutality or his irrationality.

Needless to say, the writer of this Study had made no progress towards reading the cruel riddle of Mankind's crimes and follies by the time when he was forced down from the heights of Mistrà by the twofold pressure of hunger and nightfall. Yet, before his reluctant descent, the binocular historical vision which he had acquired from a Late Medieval Italian classical education at Winchester and Oxford had won from the Laconian landscape an intuition that was the germ of the present work.

As he brooded over the catastrophe through which a Sparta founded under the auspices of a Bavarian king of Greece had usurped the role of a Mistrà that had been founded by a French prince of the Morea, it was borne in upon him that the nineteenth century performance of this historical tragedy was not the only one within his knowledge. After all, every Western schoolboy knew that the present town of Sparta was not the first to have occupied that site and borne that famous name; and, indeed, only yesterday the dreamer himself had been taking cognizance of one corner of an Hellenic Sparta which had recently been excavated by other members of the British Archaeological School at Athens. "Dorian" hands had anticipated Modern Greek hands in founding "the city on the sown-land" (sparta) at some date perhaps little less than three thousand years earlier than A.D. 1834. But if the history of a latter-day Western Society into which the Modern Greeks had forced their way out of an Ottoman prison-house was an antitype of the history of an antecedent Hellenic Civilization—and this was the aspect in which the Western Society history presented itself to an Hellenically-educated Western mind—then the Hellenic

Sparta that was the historic counterpart of the present city in the plain must be presumed to have been preceded by some pre-Hellenic counterpart of the Frankish and Ottoman Mistrà on whose topmost pinnacle the latter-day Western classical scholar was at this moment perched. An Hellenic Sparta's fortunes must have been founded on some previously regnant hill-town's catastrophe.

Had Hellenic Sparta in truth had such a predecessor? And, if so, where was the hill on which this hapless victim of that Hellenic Sparta had been set? "A city that is set on a hill cannot be hid." "I will lift up mine eyes unto the hills, from whence cometh my help"; and, raising his eyes as these texts shot through his mind, the gazer saw staring him in the face, on the crown of the bluff that overhung the farther bank of the Eurotas just opposite the all but coincident sites of Sparta the First and Sparta the Second, a monument that signalled to him the location of the pre-Hellenic counterpart of the Frankish and Otto-man citadel over whose battlements he was looking. That white masonry that was flashing over there like a helio-graph in the sunlight was "the Menelaiön" to which he had hastened to make his pilgrimage upon his arrival at Sparta three days back; and this ruined shrine was reputed to stand on the site of Therapnê, the hill-city that was said to have been the capital of Laconia in a Mycenaean last phase of Minoan history. Here, at a strategic point equiv-alent to Mistrà's situation on the opposite side of the vale, had stood Frankish Mistrà's pre-Hellenic double whose overthrow had made the first Sparta's fortune; and the historic tragedy of Mistrà had thus in truth been played at least twice in this rock-bound amphitheatre of everlasting hills.

Before the gazer descended from Mistrà that night, the impact of the Laconian landscape on his classical Weltan-

schauung had impressed on his mind two lasting lessons—
one concerning the historical geography of Continental
European Greece and the other concerning the morphology of the history of civilizations.

He had learnt that, in this Mediterranean peninsula, the
physical environment lent itself to two possible alternative
social and political régimes which had in fact alternated
with one another here at least twice over. The lie of the
land and the set of an insinuating sea had decreed that in
this country there should be a perpetual tug-of-war
between the shepherds in the highlands which covered all
but a fraction of the terra firma and the husbandmen,
artisans, and mariners in the fruitful patches of plain and
in the profitably situated ports; and the fluctuations in
a perpetual struggle between these two elements in the
population, who divided the territory so unevenly between them, were bound to be reflected in corresponding
fluctuations in the fortunes of geographical sites and in
the currency of political institutions. When the seafaring
and farming population of the ports and plains was on the
defensive—as it was apt to be particularly when it consisted of alien intruders who had thrust their way in from
overseas—it could do no more than maintain a precarious
hold over the plains, and over the passes leading from one
plain to another, from fortified eyries. One such eyrie had
been planted on the pinnacle of Mistrà by Frankish invaders in the thirteenth century of the Christian Era, and
another on the bluff at Therapnê by Minoan invaders in
the second millennium B.C., and the eventual catastrophe
in which both these variations on the same historical
theme had ended was manifestly the denouement that was
to be expected from the inherent insecurity of this type
of régime.

The exotic castle might pass, time and again, from one

set of alien hands to another—as Mistrà had passed through French, Byzantine, Ottoman, Venetian, and, once again, Ottoman hands, and Therapnê through Cretan, Pelopid, and Achaean—but, sooner or later, the tour de force was likely to end in the same way. The perilously exposed outpost of an alien civilization would be overwhelmed by a social cataclysm in which the native wild highlanders, who had been kept at bay by the intruders without ever being either subjugated or assimilated, would descend upon the plains in a devastating spate; and this recurrent catastrophe, whenever it occurred, would be apt to result in a peripeteia that would inaugurate a spell of the alternative regime. For, when once the native highlanders had thus possessed—or repossessed—themselves of the plains, the ports, and the passes, their children would come to adopt the corresponding agricultural and maritime way of life without ceasing to be a match in warfare for their cousins who had stayed among the mountains to continue there to pursue the highlanders' two traditional avocations of shepherding and brigandage. In contrast to the alien intruders from overseas, the native highlanders who had ousted them from the plains, and who, in consequence, had taken to husbandry, manufacture, and seafaring, would have it in them to break the residual wild highlanders' spirit; and the visible symbol of the effective ascendancy that, under this indigenous regime, would be established over conservative highland shepherds by ci-devant highlanders who had now become lowlanders and husbandmen, would be the replacement of a fortified citadel of Therapnê or a fortified citadel of Mistrà by an open city on "the sown-land"—a Sparta that could dispense with city-walls because the martial prowess of her disciplined citizen soldiers would have effectively struck terror into the cowed surviving highlanders' hearts.

This lesson in the historical geography of Greece which the writer had learnt on the citadel of Mistrà on the 23rd May, 1912, had been treasured by him ever since; yet it had not proved so valuable for this then still unconscious future purposes as the simultaneous lesson in the morphology of the history of civilizations. A notion of the philosophical contemporaneity and philosophical equivalence of chronologically noncontemporary representatives of this species of Society had, it is true, been implanted in his mind by his Hellenic classical education, and this tentative idea was to be ripened into conviction, little more than two years later, by the light that was to be thrown for him upon the vocabulary and the psychology of Thucydides by the outbreak of a First Western World War. Yet these influences from the social milieu into which a classically-educated post-Modern Western historian had been born might not have availed, by themselves, to initiate him into a synoptic view of History if this synoptic view had not unfolded itself physically before his eyes from the summit of Mistrà on the 23rd May, 1912, in an experience that had been personal to the spectator.

The gift of seeing relations and analogies, of bringing together into a pattern what looked at first isolated, is the high gift of the philosopher of history. If the tone of the historical insight at Mistrà was that of the historian, the tone of the following passage is that of the prophet, looking into the past as well as into the future. Here Arnold Toynbee claims to have experienced an almost mystical intuition across the gulf of ages. Six times, he tells us in the tenth volume of the *Study of History*, a vision was granted to him and he was rapt in a momentary communion with the actors of certain events in the past. There followed, however, another experience in which all temporal and spatial barriers fell, and he found himself in communion with all men and women at all times, at the center of the human psyche.

In London in the southern section of the Buckingham Palace Road, walking southward along the pavement skirting the west wall of Victoria Station, the writer, once, one afternoon not long after the end of the First World War—he had failed to record the exact date—had found himself in communion, not just with this or that episode in History, but with all that had been, and was, and was to come. In that instant he was directly aware of the passage of History gently flowing through him in a mighty current, and of his own life welling like a wave in the flow of this vast tide. The experience lasted long enough for him to take visual note of the Edwardian red brick surface and white stone facings of the station wall gliding past him on his left, and to wonder—half amazed and half amused—why this incongruously prosaic scene should have been the physical setting of a mental illumination. An instant later, the communion had ceased, and the dreamer was back again in the everyday cockney world which was his native social milieu and of which the Edwardian station wall was a characteristic period piece.

ALFRED THAYER MAHAN

(1840–1914)

When Captain Alfred Thayer Mahan in 1890 published *The Influence of Sea Power on History*, the effect was immediate and tremendous. What he actually had "discovered" was that whoever is master of the seas is master of events. Surely this was nothing new. And yet the formulation of that truth, or truism, struck his contemporaries with the force of a new idea. One commentator remarked that sea power, like oxygen, has influenced the world through the ages, but just as the nature and power of oxygen remained unrealized until Priestley, "so might sea power but for Mahan." Karl Jaspers, speaking of analogous cases in philosophy, points out that "the originality

SOURCE: Alfred Thayer Mahan, *From Sail to Steam* (New York: Harper & Brothers, 1907). Selection below reprinted by permission of Harper & Row, Inc.

of an idea often lies in the thinker's sudden insight, perhaps caused by something he is studying or something he has read and since forgotten."

I cannot now reconstitute from memory the sequence of my mental processes; but while my problem was still wrestling with my brain there dawned upon me one of those concrete perceptions which turn inward darkness into light—give substance to shadow. The Wachusett was lying at Callao, the seaport of Lima, as dull a coast town as one could dread to see. Lima being but an hour distant, we frequently spent a day there; the English Club extending to us its hospitality. In its library was Mommsen's *History of Rome*, which I gave myself to reading, especially the Hannibalic episode. It suddenly struck me, whether by some chance phrase of the author I do not know, how different things might have been could Hannibal have invaded Italy by sea, as the Romans often had Africa, instead of by the long land route; or could he, after arrival, have been in free communication with Carthage by water. This clew, once laid hold of, I followed up in the particular instance. It and the general theory already conceived threw on each other reciprocal illustration; and between the two my plan was formed by the time I reached home, in September, 1885. I would investigate coincidently the general history and naval history of the past two centuries, with a view to demonstrating the influence of the events of the one upon the other. Original research was not within my scope, nor was it necessary to the scheme thus outlined.

He who seeks, finds, if he does not lose heart; and to me, continuously seeking, came from within the suggestion that control of the sea was an historic factor which had never been systematically appreciated and expounded.

Once formulated consciously, this thought became the nucleus of all my writing for twenty years then to come; and here I may state at once what I conceive to have been my part in popularizing, perhaps in making effective, an argument for which I could by no means claim the rights of discovery. Not to mention other predecessors, with the full roll of whose names I am even now unacquainted, Bacon and Raleigh, three centuries before, had epitomized in a few words the theme on which I was to write volumes. That they had done so was, indeed, then unknown to me. For me, as for them, the light dawned first on my inner consciousness; I owed it to no other man. It has since been said by more than one that no claim for originality could be allowed me; and that I wholly concede. What did fall to me was, that no one since those two great Englishmen had undertaken to demonstrate their thesis by an analysis of history, attempting to show from current events, through a long series of years, precisely what influence the command of the sea had had upon definite issues; in brief, a concrete illustration. In the preface to my first work on the subject, for the success of which I was quite unprepared, I stated this as my aim: "An estimate of the effect of Sea Power upon the course of history and prosperity of nations; . . . resting upon a collection of special instances, in which the precise effect had been made clear by an analysis of the conditions at the given moments." This field had been left vacant, yielding me my opportunity; and concurrently therewith, untouched from the point of view proposed by me, there lay the whole magnificent series of events constituting maritime history since the days of Raleigh and Bacon, after the voyages of Columbus and Da Gama gave the impetus to over-sea activities, colonies, and commerce, which distinguishes the past three hundred years. Even of this limited period I have occupied but a part, though I fear I have skimmed the cream of that which it offers; but back behind it lie virgin fields, in the careers of the Italian republics, and others yet more remote in time, which can never be for me to narrate, although I have examined them attentively.

There are those who maintain that the pattern of ideas to which Mahan gave such persuasive expression in 1890 had been the product of ten years of vigorous discussions. Did he perhaps draft certain passages of the Naval debates? Or did he draw from a common fund of ideas for which the time was simply ripe? It is probable that his discovery would have gone unnoticed, had not the zeitgeist been propitious for its reception. As it happened, the mood was one of national pride: Americans had embarked on the path of destiny, and on that path there could be no turning. Thus Mahan's codification became the working test for the expansionists, his personal contribution to the heady ideology of imperialism. "Manifest destiny" was in the air and Mahan became its prophet.

AUGUSTINE OF HIPPO

(354–430)

Augustine wrote perhaps the first true autobiography in the
modern sense of the word. It is all there: the intense intro-
spection, the constant questioning, the prodigious understanding of false and hidden motives. Never before had a man bared
his innermost self quite like this. He didn't care what he said.
And yet—and here he differs from some of our contemporaries
—he did not wallow in his state. Driven by strong impulses he
underwent several radical transformations. At nineteen he read
Cicero's *Hortensius* which enflamed his love of philosophy.
But the encounter with Manichaean-Gnostic pseudo-knowl-
edge brought him nothing but disillusionment. For years, he

SOURCE: St. Augustine, *The Confessions*. Translated by F. V. Sheed.
(New York: Sheed & Ward, 1950). Selection below reprinted by
permission of Sheed & Ward.

tells us, he was unable to grasp that the real could be anything but a body. Finally it was Plotinus who enabled him to take the great step: to discern a purely spiritual reality where before he had conceived of God as extended in space. It was not a mere process of reasoning that led him to this insight. If we turn to the accounts given by creative people we find almost invariably an element of passivity and dependence. No matter how intense the intellectual effort that absorbed him beforehand, the moment of vision seemed to require an almost blind surrender to something other than himself.

> But you caressed my head, though I knew it not, and closed my eyes that I should not see vanity; and I ceased from myself a little and found sleep from my madness. And from that sleep I awakened in You, and I saw You infinite in a different way; but that sight was not with the eyes of the flesh.

What an inimitable description! In one instant he saw what he had not seen before—the transformation, as by magic, of a whole way of thinking. One is reminded of Michelangelo's deeply moving fresco of St. Paul gaining spiritual sight. Now his name for reality was *veritas*. And for him truth was to be known, not by looking out nor yet by looking within, but by looking above, where in an immutable light men contemplate the eternal reason of things.

> And I marvelled to find that at last I loved You and not some phantom instead of You; yet I did not stably enjoy my God, but was ravished to You by Your beauty, yet soon was torn away from You again by my own weight, and fell again with torment to lower things. Carnal habit was that weight. Yet the memory of You remained with

me and I knew without doubt that it was You to whom I should cleave, though I was not yet such as could cleave to You: for the corruptible body is a load upon the soul, and the earthly habitation presses down the mind that muses upon many things. I was altogether certain that Your invisible things are clearly seen from the creation of the world, being understood by the things that are made: so too are Your everlasting power and Your Godhead. I was now studying the ground of my admiration for the beauty of bodies, whether celestial or of earth, and what by authority I might rightly judge of things mutable and say: "This ought to be so, that not so." Enquiring then what was the source of my judgment, when I did so judge I had discovered the immutable and true eternity of truth above my changing mind. Thus by stages I passed from bodies to the soul which uses the body for its perceiving, and from this to the soul's inner power, to which the body's senses present external things, as indeed the beasts are able; and from there I passed on to the reasoning power, to which is referred for judgment what is received from the body's senses. This too realized that it was mutable in me, and rose to its own understanding. It withdrew my thought from its habitual way, abstracting from the confused crowds of fantasms that it might find what light suffused it, when with utter certainty it cried aloud that the immutable was to be preferred to the mutable, and how it had come to know the immutable itself: for if it had not come to some knowledge of the immutable, it could not have known it as certainly preferable to mutable. Thus in the thrust of a trembling glance my mind arrived at That Which Is. Then indeed I saw clearly Your invisible things which are understood by the things that are made; but I lacked the strength to hold my gaze fixed, and my weakness was beaten back again so that I returned to my old habits, bearing nothing with me but a memory of delight and a desire as for something of which I had caught the fragrance but which I had not yet the strength to eat."

The process was, of course, not to come to an end till Augustine's conversion at Cassiciacum (and even that was only a beginning), but the joyous moment of philosophical certainty laid the foundation of an utterly new future.

BLAISE PASCAL

(*1623–1662*)

Pascal was one of those who had seen the burning bush. Not that the flash of spiritual insight which he recorded in the *Memorial* should be considered a mystical experience; not if by mysticism one means either the experience of union with the Godhead or a concrete supersensory vision. It was, nevertheless, an experience that shook him to the roots of his being. Luckily for us, Pascal could never entirely help watching himself out of the corner of his eye. It was that self-consciousness so characteristic of all the apostles of Port-Royal. Moreover, he possessed an experimentalist cast of mind and consequently he put down on paper, at the first possible mo-

SOURCE: Jean Mesnard, *Blaise Pascal. His Life and Works* (New York: Philosophical Library, 1952).

ment, the overpowering crisis of his soul. The variation in the size of the handwriting (Bremond printed the document in facsimile), the fragmentary nature of the thoughts, all this points to the unconscious, where, beyond the realm of concepts, true or false inspirations have their origin.

In the year of grace 1654
Monday, 23 November, the day of St. Clement
Pope and martyr and others in the Roman Martyrology
the eve of St. Chrysogonus, Martyr, and others, etc.
From about half-past ten in the evening
Till about half an hour after midnight

FIRE

God of Abraham. God of Isaac. God of Jacob
not of the philosophers and the learned.
Certitude joy certitude emotion sight joy
GOD OF JESUS CHRIST
Deum meum et Deum vostrum
John 20, 17.

Thy God shall be my God. Ruth.
forgetfulness of the world and of everything other than
    God
He can be found only in the ways taught
in the Gospel. Greatness of the human soul.
Good Father, the world has not known
Thee, but I have known Thee. John 17.

Joy   Joy   Joy and tears of joy
I have separated myself from Thee
Dereliquerunt me fontem
my God wilt Thou leave me
let me not be eternally separated from Thee
They have life eternal, they that know Thee
Sole true God and He Whom Thou hast sent

JESUS CHRIST
JESUS CHRIST
I have separated myself from Him I have fled
      renounced crucified Him
           Pascal

So ran the memorial, sewn into Pascal's clothing so that he might always have it with him. Was this a decisive experience which was to determine and dominate the rest of his life or was it merely a passing influence? It is extraordinary that one should ask the question at all: no one would dream of denying that a moment came to Buddha or to Augustine that made all the difference. But with Pascal one finds oneself wondering what precisely it was that the spiritual awakening achieved. Had a threshold been crossed beyond which things would never be the same again? The word "certitude" would definitely point to this and according to Bremond, the severe discipline which Pascal had imposed on himself ceased to be an uphill struggle, seemed, at any rate to have been made easy for him. Thereafter, Pascal dedicated his life to the defense and explanation of Christianity. What he saw with a penetrating eye was fallen nature, left without grace, weak and miserable: "L'homme n'est donc qu'un sujet plein d'erreurs ineffaçable sans la grâce." His observations on the human condition are among the most negative ever made. As a result he felt the need for a mediator most urgently. "Pascal," says Bremond, "exalte le médiateur, mais il cache, il exile Dieu." This view did not desert Pascal even when he was writing down the burning lines of the *Memorial*. Ronald Knox shrewdly observes that even here he is sufficiently master of his own thoughts to repudiate, carefully, the implication of Deism. "God of Abraham, God of Isaac, God of Jacob"; and,

having got so far, he must needs add "not of the philosophers
and the learned." It is as if two Gods existed, and he, Pascal
were determined that his petition should go to the right address; lest there should be any doubt, he goes on "God of
Jesus Christ." This last phrase, so foreign to the vocabulary
of the Church, arose no doubt from the necessity of proclaim-
ing that formal philosophy and rational theology could not
get anywhere near the heart of the finitude and fragility of
human existence.

Pascal might have shed tears of joy at this conversion but he
did not emerge into a world of serene daylight. Even after
the event he was predisposed to take the jaundiced view. And
the shattering experience which befell him on the Bridge of
Neuilly fortified his native pessimism.

> Pascal was going, according to his habit, on a public holi-
> day, for a drive to the Bridge of Neuilly with some
> friends in a carriage with four or six horses. At the part
> of the bridge which had no protective barrier at the side,
> the galloping horses got the bits in their teeth, leapt into
> the water, and would have dragged the coach after them
> if the reins had not broken.

Such is the original narrative which later writers have
greatly embellished. But the plain fact remains that Pascal was
nearly hurled down the Seine to his death. Suddenly he became aware of the possibility of death yawning like a chasm
before him. The arbitrariness and suddenness of the accident
drastically revealed to him the precariousness and contingency
of human existence.

> When I consider the short duration of my life, swallowed
> up in the eternity before and after, the little space which

I fill, and even can see, engulfed in the infinite immensity of space of which I am ignorant, and which knows me not, I am frightened, and am astonished being here rather than there, why now rather than then.

Man left homeless, haunted by a presence he can not grasp— are these not the themes of contemporary man? It was the negative insight of Pascal that sounded the premonitory note of the twentieth century.

Nietzsche
Nachla

SÖREN KIERKEGAARD

(1813–1855)

The intense self-penetration that had set in with Augustine continued down through the Christian thinkers to Pascal, Kierkegaard, and Nietzsche. Kierkegaard the great inspirer of existentialism, was one of those philosophers who was shaken to the depth of his soul. "Here I stand," he said, "like a solitary fir-tree egoistically separate and pointed upward, casting no shadow, and only the wood-dove builds its nest in the shadow of my branches." Like no one before him, he recognized the desperate plight of the self in a world of infinite

SOURCE: Sören Kierkegaard, *Concluding Unscientific Postscript.* Translated by David F. Swenson and Walter Lowrie. Copyright 1941, © 1969 Princeton University Press, Princeton Paperback 1968. Selection below reprinted by permission of Princeton University Press and the American Scandinavian Foundation.

commitments. Philosophy, he thought, with its engrossment in what is merely universal and conceptual, could not even touch upon the problems of the anxious and bewildered man of the nineteenth century. In a deceptively light-hearted passage he recalls how he arrived at his starting point as a thinker. The notion suddenly struck him that since everyone was engaged in making things easier, someone was perhaps needed to make them hard again. And so he decided to raise difficulties where others had merely glossed over them. The irony is socratic and strives to give an intimation of the hidden truth by playfulness. Just as Socrates had considered it his task to act as gadfly to the Athenians, so Kierkegaard saw himself as the great disturber of an age that had become self-satisfied by material progress and dehumanized by an empty essentialism.

It is now about four years ago that I got the notion of wanting to try my luck as an author. I remember it quite clearly; it was on a Sunday, yes, that's it, a Sunday afternoon, I was seated as usual, out-of-doors at the Café in the Frederiksberg Garden, that wonderful garden which for the child was fairyland, where the King dwelt with his Queen, that delightful garden which for the youth was his happy diversion in the joyful merriment of the people, where now for the man of riper years there is such a homely feeling, a sad exaltation above the world and all that is of the world, where even the envied glory of the royal dignity has faded to what is indeed out there, a queen's remembrance of her deceased Lord. There I sat as usual and smoked a cigar. Unfortunately, the only resemblance I have been able to discover between the beginning of my bit of philosophic effort and the miraculous beginning of that poetical hero is the fact that it was a public resort. For the rest there is no resemblance whatever, and notwithstanding I am the author of the *Frag-*

ments, I am so insignificant that I stand outside of literature, have not even contributed to increase literature on the subscription plan, nor can with truth affirm that I occupy an important place in it.

I had been a student for half a score of years. Although never lazy, all my activity was nevertheless like a glittering inactivity, a kind of occupation for which I still have a great partiality, and for which perhaps I even have a little genius. I read much, spent the remainder of the day idling and thinking, or thinking and idling, but that was all it came to; the earliest sproutings of my productivity barely sufficed for my daily use and were consumed in their first greening. An inexplicable persuasive power constantly held me back, by strength as well as by artifice. This power was my indolence. It is not like the impetuous inspiration of love, nor like the strong prompting of enthusiasm, it is rather like a housekeeper who holds one back, with whom one is very well off, so well off that it never occurs to one to get married. So much at least is certain, that although I am not unacquainted with the comforts and conveniences of life, of all conveniences indolence is the most comfortable.

So there I sat and smoked my cigar until I lapsed into thought. Among other thoughts I remember these: "You are going on," I said to myself, "to become an old man, without being anything, and without really undertaking to do anything: On the other hand, wherever you look about you, in literature and in life, you see the celebrated names and figures, the precious and much heralded men who are coming into prominence and are much talked about, the many benefactors of the age who know how to benefit mankind by making life easier and easier, some by railways, others by omnibuses and steamboats, others by the telegraph, others by easily apprehended compendiums

and short recitals of everything worth knowing, and
finally the true benefactors of the age who make spiritual
existence in virtue of thought easier and easier, yet more
and more significant. And what are you doing?" Here my
soliloquy was interrupted, for my cigar was smoked
out and a new one had to be lit. So I smoked again, and
then suddenly this thought flashed through my mind:
"You must do something, but inasmuch as with your
limited capacities it will be impossible to make anything
easier than it has become, you must, with the same
humanitarian enthusiasm as the others, undertake to make
something harder." The notion pleased me immensely,
and at the same time it flattered me to think that I, like
the rest of them, would be loved and esteemed by the
whole community. For when all combine in every way to
make everything easier, there remains only one possible
danger, namely, that the ease becomes so great that it becomes altogether too great; then there is only one want
left, though it is not yet a felt want, when people will
want difficulty. Out of love for mankind, and out of
despair at my embarrassing situation, seeing that I had accomplished nothing and was unable to make anything
easier than it had already been made, and moved by a
genuine interest in those who make everything easy, I
conceived it as my task to create difficulties everywhere.

SUGGESTIONS FOR FURTHER READING

A massive work, the result of years of study and the triumph of a uniquely penetrating intelligence is *Insight: A Study of Human Understanding*, by Bernard Lonergan. (New York: Longmans, 1957). The author tells us that the work is not erudite. This remark should not be taken at face value. The volume is a mindstretcher and presents a challenge to any reader. The design is vast and has been carried through with the utmost care for detail, and while the design and detail make it no book to be taken to the beach on a hot summer day, it approaches the whole problem of understanding in a coherent and illuminating way. Understanding is studied as insight, the act by which we ultimately grasp the meaning of a term or the reality of a situation. The first half of the book deals with the insight of scientists, mathematicians, and men of common sense. Philosophy is concerned with a special kind of insight (an insight into insight), which establishes the validity of insights generally. The aim is not the details of what is known but the structure of the knowing mind. It is a process, he insists, "that can begin in any sufficiently cultured consciousness itself, and that leads through an understanding of all understanding to a basic understanding of all that can be understood." It is no easy going at all, yet if the subject interests one, it is an immensely rewarding work.

A reader who wishes to regard the subject of insight through the eyes of a psychologist might look into Arthur Koestler's *Insight and Outlook*. (Lincoln, Neb.: University of Nebraska Press, 1965). The insights of such men as Archimedes are reconstructed as problems in order to throw light on the mysterious achievement Koestler calls the "Eureka process." There is an interesting chapter on the interrelation between metaphor and insight.

Bertrand Russell's published work has been immense—it comprises some forty-five books. Only logicians and philosophers of science can assess his magnum opus, the *Principia Mathematica,* but his *Autobiography* (London: George Allen & Unwin Ltd., 1967) makes excellent reading and the excellence is enhanced by a superlative style. Smaller in scope and more compact is *Portraits from Memory* (New York: Simon & Schuster, 1956), in which he sketches with admirable economic restraint some of the figures and issues of his day. A reader who desires a one-volume survey of the history of Western philosophy might consult *The Wisdom of the West*. (London: MacDonald and Co., Ltd., 1960). It marches briskly from Thales to Wittgenstein and is peppered with sallies of Lord Russell's somewhat caustic wit.

The philosophy of Ludwig Wittgenstein is luminously discussed in David Pear's *Ludwig Wittgenstein*. (New York: The Viking Press, 1970). The author, himself a philosopher of standing, has done an admirable job of making Wittgenstein's thought accessible to the nonspecialist. There is a long introduction in which his thought is placed in the larger context of modern philosophy.

In spite of the complexity of Wittgenstein's nature, which at times veered towards the pathological, he wrote lighthearted and whimsical letters filled with penetrating insights. These gems are included in Professor Norman Malcolm's short and perfect *Memoir: Ludwig Wittgenstein,* with a prefatory biographical sketch by Professor George Henrik von Wright (Oxford University Press, 1958). It is a corrective to any mistaken notion that Wittgenstein was a desiccated philosopher.

Another excellent source to begin acquiring an understanding of Wittgenstein's place among the Oxford philosophers is *Fly and the Fly-Bottle* by Ved Mehta. (Boston: Little, Brown and Company, 1961). The book, subtitled *Encounters with British Intellectuals,* includes a sparkling conversation with Lord Russell whose staccato speech and caustic humor have been perfectly caught by Mr. Mehta.

The Notebooks and Papers of Gerard Manley Hopkins. (Oxford University Press, 1959). Here, edited with scrupulous care is a host of personal entries—books he read, notes for poetry, friends' addresses, reflections on himself, objects which formed his visual taste. This sense of the interconnectedness of things makes the entries so extraordinary. Over thirty of Hopkins's drawings show his intense observations of trees, intertwined foliage, rocks and plants—a conjunction he particularly liked. Fragments of early verse, music, and sketches make those miscellaneous papers invaluable for the light they shed on the man himself.

Kenneth Clark is presently the center of so much popular attention, that praising *Civilisation* (New York: Harper & Row, 1970) is carrying owls to Athens. Manner and tone of voice are different in *The Nude* (New York: Doubleday Anchor Book, 1956), a more scholarly work, but the charm is all there and so is the mental finesse.

Richard Wagner's *My Life* (New York: Dodd, Mead & Co., 1911) does not make "good reading" when the autobiography is considered as a whole. It remains, however, important for one reason—it was written by Wagner. More illuminating is *Richard Wagner an Mathilde und Otto Wesendonk* (Leipzig: Herausgegeben von Dr. Julius Kapp, Hesse & Becker, Verlag), letters which reveal much that has been carefully covered up in the autobiography. Besides, we get the minutiae of daily living that affected his creative processes so strongly.

As for old Father Parmenides, as Socrates called him, there exists a complete translation of Hermann Diels' *Fragmente der Vorsokratiker* (Kathleen Freeman: *Ancilla to the Pre-Socratic Philosophers*, Oxford: Blackwell, 1956). Those who may fiind this classic work a bit unwieldy might look into *The Presocratic Philosophers*, by G. S. Kirk. (Cambridge: Cambridge University Press, 1959). It includes discussions on controversial issues of text and interpretation.

The Pre-socratics afford a fair field for those with philosophical axes to grind. Nietzsche, who sensed the extraordinary in Parmenides, was nevertheless totally out of sympathy with his thought. Savage as his attack is, he never allows us to forget that his philosophy is of the highest importance. *The Philosophy of Nietzsche*, edited with an introduction by Geoffrey Clive (New York: Mentor Books, New American Library, 1965). It is difficult thinking but not difficult reading.

In reading Anselm we catch something of the pure spirit of Parmenides. The chief source for Anselm's life is the biographical work of his friend, disciple, and secretary, Eadmer, whose methods have much in common with those of modern biographers. *Eadmer: Life of St. Anselm, Archbishop of Canterbury*, edited with introduction, notes, and translation, by R. W. Southern (London & New York: Thomas Nelson, 1962). Better still, to read the man himself. Whoever does not wish to climb the spiral staircase leading to Migne's *Patrologia Latina* (vols. 158–9), or read the somewhat ponderous translations made in the nineteenth century, might consult *Basic Writings*, translated by Sidney Norton Deane (La Salle,

Illinois: Open Court Publishing Co., 1962). Though composed over the decades, Anselm's works fall into place like parts of a planned totality.

On Nicholas of Cusa there are two voluminous studies by Edmond Vansteenberghe, *Le Cardinal Nicholas de Cuse* (Paris: H. Champion, 1920) primarily a biography. It includes a resume of his extraordinary original system. The same author has another essay on the subject: *Autour de la docte ignorance, une controverse sur la theologic mystique au XVe siecle.* (Munster in Westphalia, 1914). The reader may, however, at times be overcome by a sense of almost impenetrable obscurity.

The recent work on Nicholas of Cusa that will dispel all such discouragement is Karl Jasper's lucid and profound study of Cusanus in *The Great Philosophers Vol. 1* (Harcourt, Brace & World, Inc.: New York, 1966). It has an inimitable philosophical tone, sustained over long passages, and conveys brilliantly the substance of his thinking, the man himself and his place in history and philosophy.

Whoever wishes to catch the flavor of the age might read the memoirs of the Cardinal's great friend and patron Enea Silvio Piccolomini: *Memoirs of a Rennaissance Pope,* by Leona Gabel (New York: Putnam, 1959). Also, *Erasmus and his Times* by Louis Bouyer (Westminster, Maryland: The Newman Press, 1959), which shows the nature of the first encounter of the spirit of medieval civilization with the new spirit of the Renaissance.

A translation that will not soon be superseded in beauty is Goethe's *Italian Journey,* translated by Elizabeth Meyer and W. H. Auden. (New York: Pantheon Books, 1962). If the work gains a permanent place in English literature, it might well be due to the skill and imagination of the translators.

If the *Phenomenon of Man* (New York: Harper & Brothers, 1959) contains the kernel of Teilhard de Chardin's scientific thought, *The Divine Milieu* (New York: Harper & Brothers, 1960) is a key to the religious meditation that accompanied it. As readers of the *Phenomenon* know Père Teilhard has a liking for abstract words and a personal scientific vocabulary. In the *Letters from a Traveller* (London: Collins, 1962), however, the personality of Teilhard comes through. No one can read these letters without mounting admiration for the singleness of his mind and heart, unspoiled by success or increasing disappointment.

Dr. Stephen Mason's *A History of the Sciences* (New York: Collier Books, 1962) is not meat for children. Before reading it, one already must have a fair knowledge of the history of science to find out how little one knows about it after all. The book's special merit lies in the account it gives of how philosophical and theological conceptions influenced scientific inquiry.

James D. Watson's somewhat flamboyant *Double Helix* (New York: Atheneum, 1968) is aimed at the general reader and gives an exciting personal account of how the author discovered the double-helical structure of deoxyribonucleic acid. (DNA). For further historical background one might turn to "The Discovery of DNA" by Alfred E. Mirsky (*Scientific American;* Vol. 218, No. 6, June 1968), where he deals fascinatingly with the pioneering work for DNA.

Economics has been called a dismal science, but Professor Robert L. Heilbroner has made the story of the great economists— a strange lot—anything but abstruse in *The Worldly Philosophers* (New York: a Clarion Book, Simon & Schuster, 1968). His knack of fastening onto what is important and of seeing what the majority miss, make his book totally absorbing to the layman.

Admiral Alfred T. Mahan's *From Sail to Steam* (New York: Harper & Brothers, 1967) was an immense success when it first appeared in 1907. One cannot but be impressed by the seriousness of the author's outlook and granted his historico-philosophical predilections, it is still to the point and interesting. Nevertheless, the measured cynicism of Barbara Tuchman's *Proud Tower* (New York: Macmillan, 1969) comes as a welcome relief. She clearly hasn't swallowed the Admiral whole. For further background the reader might consult *The Shaping of American Diplomacy*, edited with commentary by William Appleman Williams (Chicago: Rand McNally & Co., 1968), which contains an analysis of those concepts and beliefs for which Mahan became the spokesman.

No need anymore to plow through Migne's dusty volumes, since so many of Augustine's works are now available in the Ancient Christian Writers Series. Magnificent and unforgettable formulations turn up at every bend of the road and make the long journey worthwhile. The whirlwind of his thought causes him to be truly eloquent in the *Confessions* (New York: Sheed & Ward, 1943). Mr. Sheed has translated Augustine's work into faultless English but could not, of course, reproduce the assonances—at times the Latin almost sings itself. The thought of Augustine has been lucidly analyzed by Karl Jaspers: *The Great Philosophers, Vol. 1* (New York: Harcourt, Brace & World, 1966). We are allowed to share the climate of his mind and in spite of a slight bias against the Saint's character, he leaves no doubt that we are dealing with a philosopher of the highest order.

And finally, here are two important studies on the meaning and history of existentialism and its precursors: One is the *Irrational Man* by William Barrett (Garden City, N.J.: Doubleday Anchor Books, 1962). Professor Barrett knows exactly what he wants to say and says it with immense lucidity and skill. But the extent of knowledge needed to trace the movement of existentialist thought is even more impressive. Focused on a different aspect is M. C. D'Arcy's *No Absent God*. (New York: Harper & Row, 1962). Father D'Arcy is an exceedingly learned man, but he carries his learning lightly. Yet no one can portray the desperate plight of the self quite as penetratingly as he. The heart of the book is a reflection on the existentialist predicament seen through the eyes of Kierkegaard, Nietzsche, Heidegger, and Sartre.